This is an outstanding book, one of the clearest analyses of NGOs trying to influence the current world of multilevel governance. It is must reading for any student of the global trade system, the EU, and global governance in general.

Craig Murphy, Department of Conflict Resolution, Human Security, and Global Governance, The University of Massachusetts Boston, USA

Erin Hannah sheds much light on the complex role of non-governmental organizations in promoting progressive policies across integrating markets. Based on extensive research inside contemporary Europe, her accessible analysis highlights the limits of the most ambitious advocacy strategies. Pushing those limits remains possible, but success depends upon subtlety, persistence, and patience. NGO leaders, and anyone interested in their important work, should read this splendid book.

Louis W. Pauly, Professor of Political Science, University of Toronto, Canada

This important book reaches a dismal conclusion – wildly successful NGO campaigning in the EU has only marginally impacted on trade policy. But, it is not a counsel of despair – potential routes out of this global epistemic logjam are identified and elaborated. Essential reading for anyone interested in understanding the contemporary limits to NGO campaigning.

David Hulme, Professor of Development Studies, University of Manchester, UK

NGOs and Global Trade

In a deeply iniquitous world, where the gains from trade are distributed unevenly and where trade rules often militate against progressive social values, human health, and sustainable development, non-governmental organizations (NGOs) are widely touted as our best hope for redressing these conditions. As a critical voice of the poor and marginalized, many are engaged in a global struggle for democratic norms and social justice. Yet the potential for NGOs to bring about meaningful change is limited. This book examines whether improvements in participatory opportunities for progressive NGOs results in substantive and normative policy change in one of the major trading powers, the European Union (EU).

Hannah advances a constructivist account of the role of NGOs in the EU's trade policymaking process. She argues that NGOs have been instrumental in providing education, raising awareness, and giving a voice to broader societal concerns about proposed trade deals, both when they take advantage of formal participatory opportunities and when they protest from the streets and in the media. However, the book also highlights how NGO inputs are mediated by the social structure of global trade governance. Epistemes—the background knowledge, ideological and normative beliefs, and shared assumptions about how the world works—determine who has a voice in global trade governance.

Showing how NGOs succeed only when their advocacy conforms broadly to the dominant episteme, this book will be of value to scholars and students with an interest in NGOs and international trade negotiations. It will also be of interest to policymakers, national trade negotiators, government departments, and the trade policy community.

Erin Hannah is Associate Professor of Political Science at King's University College at the University of Western Ontario, Canada. She is an international political economist specializing in global governance, trade, sustainable development, poverty and inequality, global civil society, and European Union trade politics.

Global Institutions

Edited by Thomas G. Weiss
The CUNY Graduate Center, New York, USA
and Rorden Wilkinson
University of Sussex, Brighton, UK

About the series

The "Global Institutions Series" provides cutting-edge books about many aspects of what we know as "global governance." It emerges from our shared frustrations with the state of available knowledge—electronic and print-wise, for research and teaching—in the area. The series is designed as a resource for those interested in exploring issues of international organization and global governance. And since the first volumes appeared in 2005, we have taken significant strides toward filling conceptual gaps.

The series consists of three related "streams" distinguished by their blue, red, and green covers. The blue volumes, comprising the majority of the books in the series, provide user-friendly and short (usually no more than 50,000 words) but authoritative guides to major global and regional organizations, as well as key issues in the global governance of security, the environment, human rights, poverty, and humanitarian action among others. The books with red covers are designed to present original research and serve as extended and more specialized treatments of issues pertinent for advancing understanding about global governance. And the volumes with green covers—the most recent departure in the series—are comprehensive and accessible accounts of the major theoretical approaches to global governance and international organization.

The books in each of the streams are written by experts in the field, ranging from the most senior and respected authors to first-rate scholars at the beginning of their careers. In combination, the three components of the series—blue, red, and green—serve as key resources for faculty, students, and practitioners alike. The works in the blue and green streams have value as core and complementary readings in courses on, among other things, international organization, global governance, international law, international relations, and international political economy; the red volumes allow further reflection and investigation in these and related areas.

The books in the series also provide a segue to the foundation volume that offers the most comprehensive textbook treatment available dealing with all the major issues, approaches, institutions, and actors in contemporary global governance—our edited work *International Organization and Global Governance* (2014)—a volume to which many of the authors in the series have contributed essays.

Understanding global governance—past, present, and future—is far from a finished journey. The books in this series nonetheless represent significant steps toward a better way of conceiving contemporary problems and issues as well as, hopefully, doing something to improve world order. We value the feedback from our readers and their role in helping shape the on-going development of the series.

A complete list of titles appears at the end of this book. The most recent titles in the series are:

NGOs and Global Trade (2016)
by Erin Hannah

Brazil as a Rising Power (2016)
edited by Kai Michael Kenkel and Philip Cunliffe

Summits and Regional Governance (2015)
edited by Gordon Mace, Jean-Philippe Thérien, Diana Tussie, and Olivier Dabène

Global Consumer Organizations (2015)
by Karsten Ronit

World Trade Organization (2nd edition, 2015)
by Bernard M. Hoekman and Petros C. Mavroidis

Women and Girls Rising (2015)
by Ellen Chesler and Terry McGovern

The North Atlantic Treaty Organization (2nd edition, 2015)
by Julian Lindley-French

NGOs and Global Trade

Non-state voices in EU
trade policymaking

Erin Hannah

Routledge
Taylor & Francis Group

LONDON AND NEW YORK

First published 2016 by Routledge

2 Park Square, Milton Park, Abingdon, Oxfordshire OX14 4RN

711 Third Avenue, New York, NY 10017

Routledge is an imprint of the Taylor & Francis Group, an informa business

First issuedinpaperback2017

British Library Cataloguing in Publication Data
A catalogue record for this book is available from the British Library

Library of Congress Cataloging in Publication Data
A catalog record for this book has been requested

ISBN: 978-0-415-71263-7 (hbk)
ISBN: 978-1-138-47764-3 (pbk)

Typeset in Times New Roman
by Taylor & Francis Books

For Nan,
ever present in my heart

Contents

List of illustrations

Acknowledgement

I would like to acknowledge the many individuals and institutions whose assistance and support helped me to complete this book. I would like to thank the editors of the Global Institutions Series, Thomas G. Weiss and Rorden Wilkinson, for their extraordinary mentorship. They saw promise in turning these ideas into a book long before I did. Their encouragement instilled in me the confidence to take the bushel off the light—for that I am eternally grateful.

The University of Toronto, King's University College at the University of Western Ontario, and the Social Sciences and Humanities Research Council (SSHRC) generously provided research funding that made it possible to conduct field research in Brussels and Geneva over several years. I am particularly grateful to my home institution, King's University College, for providing me the resources, intellectual space, and time to complete this book. I also owe a debt of gratitude to the Brooks World Poverty Institute at the University of Manchester, the Johan Skytte Foundation at Uppsala University, and the Department of Political and Economic Studies at the University of Helsinki, which made it possible for me to attend workshops in South Africa, Sweden, and Finland to exchange ideas with the world's foremost thinkers on global trade and development.

I have been blessed to work with the gifted Amy Wood. A rising star in her own right, Amy provided first-rate research assistance for this book. In addition to conducting research, copy-editing, idea-bouncing, and wrestling the manuscript into shape, Amy provided incredibly helpful feedback on several drafts. The quality of her insights and work ethic astonish me.

I want to thank Louis W. Pauly and Steven Bernstein for their invaluable guidance and advice over many years. Grace Skogstad, Amy Verdun, and Jeffery Kopstein also provided extensive feedback on earlier drafts of the manuscript. Their suggestions lent depth and clarity to the project. I am also thankful to Nicola Parkin, Lydia DeCruz, and the team at Routledge for all their exemplary work. It has been an absolute pleasure to work with them all.

This book would not have been possible without the influence, constructive feedback, decisive interventions, and boundless enthusiasm of my friends and collaborators, James Scott, Silke Trommer, and Rorden Wilkinson. Whether we are "talking trade" in Cape Town, Bali, Geneva, Uppsala, Helsinki, Nairobi or anywhere in between, these brilliant minds push me to think outside the box about how trade can be leveraged in the global fight against poverty. They have each had a profound impact on this book and are a constant source of inspiration. I would also like to thank my dear friends and colleagues at King's— Tozun Bahcheli, Graham Broad, Renée Soulodre-La France, and Thomas Tieku—who have sustained me over the years with laughter, long talks, and many, many fine meals.

Most of all, I am grateful for my wonderful, growing family who show me every day what matters most. Thank you to Mauro and Sydney Facchin for anchoring my heart and filling my life with love and happiness.

Erin Hannah
London, Canada
July 2015

Abbreviations

ACT UP	AIDS Coalition to Unleash Power
AIDS	acquired immunodeficiency syndrome
ARV	antiretroviral
BEUC	Bureau Européen des Unions de Consommateurs
CCBE	Council of Bars and Law Societies of Europe
CCP	Common Commercial Policy
CEEP	Centre of Enterprises with Public Participation and of Enterprises of General Economic Interest
CEO	Corporate Europe Observatory
CETA	Comprehensive Economic Trade Agreement
CGE	Computer Generated Equilibrium
CIDSE	Coopération Internationale pour le Développement et la Solidarité
COGECA	Comité Général de la Coopération Agricole de l'Union Européenne
COPA	Comité des Organisations Professionnelles Agricoles de l'Union Européenne
COREPER	Committee of Permanent Representatives
CPTECH	Consumer Project on Technology
CSD	Civil Society Dialogue
DDA	Doha Development Agenda
DG	Directorate-General
DSU	Dispute Settlement Understanding
EC	European Community
ECI	European Citizens' Initiative
ECJ	European Court of Justice
EEA	European Express Association
EESC	European Economic and Social Committee
EFPIA	European Federation of Pharmaceutical Industries and Associations

EFTA	European Foreign Trade Association
EGA	European Generics Association
EP	European Parliament
EPA	Economic Partnership Agreement
EPHA	European Public Health Alliance
EPSU	European Federation of Public Service Unions
ERT	European Roundtable of Industrialists
ESC	European and Social Committee
ESF	European Services Forum
ETUC	European Trade Union Confederation
EU	European Union
FOE	Friends of the Earth
FTA	free trade agreement
GATS	General Agreement on Trade in Services
GATT	General Agreement on Tariffs and Trade
HAI	Health Action International
HIV	human immunodeficiency virus
IGO	intergovernmental organization
IMF	International Monetary Fund
INTA	Committee on International Trade
IP	intellectual property
IPC	Intellectual Property Committee
IPM	Interactive Policymaking Initiative
IPR	intellectual property rights
IR	international relations
ISDS	investor-to-state dispute settlement
LDCs	least-developed countries
MAI	Multilateral Agreement on Investment
MEP	member of the European Parliament
MFN	most-favored nation
MNCs	multinational corporations
MSF	Médecins Sans Frontières/Doctors Without Borders
NGO	non-governmental organization
NTA	New Transatlantic Agenda
OECD	Organisation for Economic Co-operation and Development
OLP	Ordinary Legislative Procedure
PPIAF	Public-Private Infrastructure Advisory Facility
PPP	public-private partnership
PTA	preferential trade agreement
R&D	research and development
TABC	Trans-Atlantic Business Council

TABD	Trans-Atlantic Business Dialogue
TEC	Treaty Establishing the European Community
TEU	Treaty on European Union
TFEU	Treaty on the Functioning of the European Union
TiSA	Trade in Services Agreement
ToL	Treaty of Lisbon
TPC	Trade Policy Committee
TRIPS	Trade-Related Aspects of Intellectual Property Rights
TTIP	Transatlantic Trade and Investment Partnership
UN	United Nations
UNCTAD	United Nations Conference on Trade and Development
UNICE	Union of Industrial and Employers' Confederations of Europe
USTR	United States Trade Representative
WDM	World Development Movement
WHO	World Health Organization
WIDE	Network for Women in Development
WIPO	World Intellectual Property Organization
WTO	World Trade Organization
WWF	World Wide Fund for Nature

Introduction

International trade has been a focal point for political and social contestation since the conclusion of the Uruguay Round of Multilateral Trade Negotiations in 1994. The extension of World Trade Organization (WTO) Agreements into new areas such as investment, services, and intellectual property rights has engendered massive conflict and rendered ongoing negotiations infinitely more technical and complex. A chorus of legitimacy concerns was raised by the extension of trade rules beyond barriers to trade "at the border" to national regulatory regimes in a host of ostensibly non-trade areas such as food safety, environment, human health, and taxation. The strength of the WTO's Dispute Settlement Understanding (DSU), a system now characterized by compulsory adjudication with binding outcomes, ensures that governments no longer enjoy the same degree of practical flexibility in enforcing international trade rules. Many are concerned that this makes governments less able to regulate in the public interest.

Meanwhile, the WTO's Doha Development Round of multilateral trade negotiations is trapped in seemingly endless deadlock. Growing inequalities, deepening environmental damage and social dislocation, and stark imbalances in economic and commercial opportunities signal a failure on the part of the WTO to produce welfare gains for all. Growing suspicion by developing countries that their industrial counterparts lack serious commitment to resolve fundamental disparities and distributional issues exacerbates this situation. The "bicycle theory" narrative—the notion that ever greater market opening is needed to prevent economic crisis—continues to drive further trade liberalization through the vehicles of plurilateral and preferential trade agreements (PTAs), and threatens to ratchet up trade rules, cutting the poorest countries and their commercial interests out of rule making, and further entrenching asymmetries in the global economy.

These developments are accompanied by the proliferation of progressive non-governmental organizations (NGOs) that are critical of the global trade agenda. These actors are mobilizing, not only to ensure that particular sectors are protected or insulated from the costs of trade liberalization, but to demand that trade-related decision-making processes directly engage global civil society and that trade rules serve sustainable development priorities and reflect broader social values and purposes. They aim to elevate social, health, developmental, and environmental concerns of entire communities over market-related concerns in the international trade system and to give a voice to poor and otherwise marginalized groups in trade politics. They are engaged in a wider struggle to establish a new global ethic wherein democratic norms and social justice infuse all levels of decision-making in global economic governance. Whether more open trade policymaking processes that include progressive NGOs lead to a more legitimate and qualitatively enhanced international trade system is the central concern of this book.

The European Union (EU)[1] stands out among major trading powers for its significant and dramatic response to new demands for access and participation. Since the conclusion of the Uruguay Round, non-state actors—including economic actors such as business and industry associations and non-economic actors such as NGOs—have experienced sustained, aggregate improvements in access and participatory conditions in the external trade policymaking process.[2] This book examines whether improvements in political opportunities for progressive NGOs result in more legitimate external trade policymaking in the EU. Legitimacy is assessed along two lines: the way policy is made (procedural legitimacy), and the projected outcomes of policy (substantive legitimacy).[3] The role of NGOs is evaluated in two important cases in the context of WTO negotiations since 2000. The first concerns the formulation of the EU's position on Trade-Related Aspects of Intellectual Property Rights (TRIPS) and access to medicines. The second concerns the EU's requests for water services liberalization in the context of General Agreement on Trade in Services (GATS) negotiations.

Through a critical comparison of the role of NGOs in these cases, the book argues that there is clear potential for NGOs to represent citizens' demands, constitute a basic form of popular representation, and hold decision-makers accountable to a broader public. Indeed, in both cases, NGOs have been instrumental in providing education, raising awareness, and giving a voice to broader societal concerns about the social, environmental, and health-related aspects of proposed trade deals. However, they have not been able to determine policy outcomes in this arena, regardless of whether they are deeply and formally integrated into the trade policymaking process or protesting on the margins. This failure is owing to the robust normative framework within which the negotiations took place.

In developing this argument, the book challenges a theoretical perspective on public policymaking called cosmopolitanism. Grounded in democratic and normative theory, cosmopolitanism conceives of global civil society, and progressive NGOs in particular, as conduits for democracy and social justice in global or regional governance. Cosmopolitanism offers only partial insight into the role of NGOs because it does not adequately account for the prevailing social structure in which decisions are made. In response to these shortcomings, the book builds upon the insights of constructivism to advance an alternative account of the dynamics at play in the EU.

The book argues that the shift from the General Agreement on Tariffs and Trade (GATT) to the WTO entrenched a legal-liberal episteme in the international trade regime, thereby determining patterns of empowerment in the EU's external trade policymaking process, and ultimately hamstringing NGO efforts to influence policy outcomes. Epistemes constitute the deepest level of the ideational world and endow some with the authority to determine valid knowledge or to reproduce the knowledge on which an episteme is based. Technocrats and experts are empowered, relative to other actors, because they possess an authoritative claim on knowledge. The more technical an issue is, the more functional authority—i.e. the ability to shape the terms of debate and to initiate and execute critical decisions— pools in their hands. By working to ensure new trade rules rest on sound liberal and legal epistemic foundations, experts and technocrats serve as gatekeepers, determining who has a voice in governance. The precise role of NGOs in EU external trade policymaking is therefore determined by the fitness of their demands and grievances with the prevailing legal-liberal episteme. NGOs have succeeded only when their attempts to achieve more democratic, sustainable, and equitable trade policies have conformed broadly to the dominant episteme. When they seek to overrule that episteme, they fail. These findings suggest that early optimism about the power of NGOs to influence international public policy was both premature and naive.[4]

Addressing whether and how new political opportunities for NGOs affect trade processes and policy outcomes in the EU is important for several reasons. First, the question of the EU's legitimacy has been hotly debated for three decades because democracy, member state autonomy, and the effectiveness of supranational decision-making are perennially in tension.[5] Until the early 1990s, indirect or output legitimacy were seen as adequate bases for authoritative decision-making.[6] In the case of the former, it was commonly agreed that the legitimacy of the EU was domestically authorized by, and originated from, the authority of member states—legitimation was derived from an agreement of member states as well as the permission of citizens of these states to participate in the EU through referendum.[7] Thus, policy outputs are indirectly legitimated when they reflect state preferences. In terms of output legitimacy, scholars conceive of the EU as a problem-solving agency or technocratic "fourth branch of government" which produces outputs that are pareto-efficient, rather than redistributive or value-allocative. In order to achieve output legitimacy, regulatory policy-making by supranational institutions is intentionally isolated from the democratic process or capture by majoritarian interests.[8] However, few scholars or policymakers still defend output legitimacy as an adequate basis of authority.[9]

The Single European Act (1986) and the Maastricht Treaty (1992) moved the EU towards a political system in its own right and it became clear that a system based on indirect legitimation was not conducive to deeper integration or even the smooth day-to-day functioning of the EU. The ratification crises that followed in 1992, 2001, 2005, and 2008 highlighted public concern over the legitimation of EU power. Qualified majority voting and an increase in the delegation of exclusive competence from national to supranational institutions in sensitive issue areas made it more difficult to claim legitimacy in the EU on the basis of efficiency or performance alone.[10]

In the absence of social legitimacy or, rather, a well-developed and identifiable "European people,"[11] the focus has shifted towards input or procedural legitimacy as a necessary basis for authoritative rule making in the EU.[12] Input or procedural legitimation strategies take democratic norms of public participation and control as indispensable features of legitimate governance. Essentially, these strategies attempt to democratize the processes by which EU-level policy is formed. This may be achieved by enhancing the representation of citizen demands in EU institutions[13] and by injecting more direct participatory mechanisms and/or deliberative democracy into EU decision-making, with the aim of constructing a sense of collective identity or political will.[14] The improvements in access and participatory conditions for non-state actors in the external trade policymaking process are outgrowths of these imperatives and are therefore deserving of scholarly attention if we are to better understand the conditions under which EU governance may be legitimated.

In addition, striking an appropriate balance between inclusive channels of participation and access on one hand and efficient policymaking on the other is a challenge encountered by all major WTO powers. For Martin and Goldstein, there are distinct dangers associated with the shift from GATT to WTO. In particular, greater legal precision of trade rules and increased availability of information about the distributional consequences of proposed agreements tends to increase the incentives for those negatively affected by the rules to mobilize and demand their interests are translated into policy.[15] The tension between demands for participation and efficient policymaking is amplified by the fact that the effective inclusion of actors who view trade liberalization critically could serve to undermine the free trade imperative, one of the original rationales underpinning the creation of the EU. Conversely, the systematic exclusion or marginalization of these groups seriously calls into question the legitimacy of the trade policymaking process. Therefore, the shift from GATT to WTO is not only important for its distributional consequences regarding which sectors or firms benefit, but now also has broader implications for whether trade policy reflects wider societal interests, demands, and concerns. This book sheds light on the ways in which the EU navigates these dynamics and tensions, and reflects upon the lessons that could be shared with other WTO members.

More broadly, the book contributes to the massive literature on the emergence and role of NGOs in international politics.[16] The wide-ranging impact of NGOs on global governance[17] and on the establishment, dissemination, and enforcement of global norms,[18] in the areas of human rights,[19] environment,[20] landmines,[21] and women's rights[22] amongst many others, has been the subject of extensive inquiry. A common denominator is the view that NGOs can and do represent global citizens' demands, constitute a basic form of popular representation, and can hold decision-makers to account, especially through "naming and shaming" tactics.[23] This book advances our understanding of the role of NGOs in international politics by redressing several problems prevalent in the literature.

First, there is a tendency for scholars to focus either on the role of NGOs in international organizations or to adopt "second image reversed" perspectives.[24] With respect to global trade, the public campaigns waged by NGOs and their potential to improve the democratic accountability of the WTO have been focal points for research.[25] By conceiving of international trade politics as either one- or two-level games, scholars tend to neglect the host of opportunities for NGO influence below the state at both the local and regional levels.[26] This book considers the multi-level environment in which NGOs in global trade operate and the ways in which NGOs interact with local-, regional-, and national-level decision-makers.

Second, research on the impact of NGOs in international public policymaking has been widely criticized for conflating correlation between prevalent NGO activity and policy change with causation. Drezner, for example, points to research on the role of NGOs in the negotiation of multilateral environmental agreements and the Multilateral Agreement on Investment (MAI) to highlight scholars' tendency to ignore alternative explanations for policy change and to blur "public activity with causal effect."[27] With respect to global trade specifically, comparative research on NGOs in the international trade regime is scarce and the focus tends to be on specific episodes of peak activity or "easy tests" where they are most likely to thrive.[28] Therefore, scholars have had difficulty specifying scope conditions for when NGOs are likely to succeed in altering outcomes in international trade negotiations. By contrast, this book considers several alternative accounts of the role of NGOs in the EU's external trade policymaking process and conducts rigorous process tracing and comparative case studies.

Third, there is a paucity of research on the role of NGOs in the EU's external trade policymaking process despite the burgeoning body of literature focusing on the role of global civil society in Europe and the evolving political opportunity structure for non-state actors at the EU level.[29] Scholars highlight the pervasiveness of NGO influence in areas such as food safety and environment in the EU,[30] while numerous other case studies show that the quality of NGO influence and participation tends to deteriorate at the policy implementation stage across a range of issue areas including human rights, asylum seeking,[31] and social policy.[32] Nonetheless, the role of NGOs in EU trade policymaking has received little attention.

This gap in the literature is puzzling for several reasons. First, the EU has primary competency for negotiating international trade agreements.[33] Second, the expanded scope and extension of trade rules into ostensibly non-trade areas such as food safety and public health, and the dis-embedding of markets from broader societal and environmental values are focal points for concern amongst NGOs. Third, the highly technical and legalized nature of international trade rules render this a unique domain in which to study NGO influence. Fourth, the NGOs operating in this issue area are among the most highly mobilized and well-resourced in the EU. Finally, it is widely believed that more open trade policymaking processes that include NGOs will, by virtue of the divergence of interests represented, lead to a stronger, more legitimate, and qualitatively enhanced international trade system.[34] Yet, as noted above, there has been little empirical research on the ways in which NGO influence is channeled upward through local, regional, and national levels of governance in WTO members.

The notable exception to this vacancy in the EU literature is offered by Dür and De Bièvre who examine the influence of NGOs in negotiations concerning the European Partnership Agreements (EPAs) and the EU's policy on access to medicines in developing countries.[35] The authors argue that newly mobilized NGOs enjoy greater inclusion in the external trade policymaking process than in previous periods but have had little influence over policy outcomes in these areas because they have diffuse costs and benefits from trade policies. In Dür and De Bièvre's view, NGOs lack sufficient information about constituency preferences or market conditions to advance persuasive positions; they are unable to hold policymakers accountable by threatening their chance of re-election or reappointment; they are only able to mount flash campaigns; and they advance extreme positions that are virtually impossible to achieve.

This is a welcome addition to the literature on NGO influence in the EU's external trade policymaking process and, as I discuss in Chapter 4, I share the view that NGOs were ultimately unsuccessful in determining policy outcomes in this area. However, a closer examination of the various stages of policy development suggests that Dür and De Bièvre miss important dynamics in the external trade policymaking process. Indeed, they do not adequately account for variable patterns of empowerment. The authors argue that business and trade associations will be more successful than NGOs in providing detailed and precise information, and that NGOs will be active during the agenda-setting stage while business associations will successfully shape policy outcomes. The authors neglect to consider the important role played by experts and technocrats in this process and the extent to which firms and business associations may also be sidelined in the policy development stages. Furthermore, the authors imply that well-resourced NGOs who hold considerable information about market conditions and the practical impact of new rules on the ground, who are willing to compromise with policymakers, and who advance moderate policy proposals are likely to be successful in influencing policy outcomes in the EU's external trade policymaking process.

This book calls these assumptions into question and Chapters 3 and 4 show that there is more at work than diffuse costs and benefits arising from trade policies. In order to understand why some actors have a voice and others are silenced in trade negotiations we require a deeper understanding of the social structure in which these negotiations take place.[36] It is the central claim of this book that epistemes structure patterns of empowerment, and enable and delimit agency in global trade, and in the EU's external trade policymaking process specifically.

How the argument unfolds

Theoretical markers

This book evaluates whether improvements in access and participatory conditions for progressive NGOs result in more legitimate external trade policymaking in the EU. In order to study the evolving role of NGOs in trade politics and to explain patterns of empowerment in the EU's external trade policymaking process, Chapter 1 establishes the theoretical framework for the book. First, the chapter details a working conception of legitimacy. A post-national, principled conception of legitimacy based in the cosmopolitan international relations (IR) literature is developed to serve as a benchmark for the analysis. Cosmopolitanism expects that increasing participation and improved political opportunities for NGOs should lead to improved legitimacy of policymaking along both procedural and substantive lines. The chapter then draws insight from constructivism to develop an alternative and competing account of the role of NGOs in the trade policymaking process. This framework builds upon a broad conceptualization of episteme based in Foucault's work,[37] adapted to IR and made amenable to empirical research by Adler and Bernstein.[38] According to this account, tensions are created when NGO mandates conflict with the widely held norms, consensual scientific knowledge, and ideological beliefs that underpin the prevailing episteme. NGO efforts to ensure that new trade rules elevate social, health, developmental, and environmental concerns over market-related concerns are effectively hamstrung by the robust liberal and legal epistemic foundations of the international trade regime, both when they participate formally in trade policymaking and when they protest from the margins. Therefore the question of whether improvements in access and participatory conditions improve legitimacy hinges on the "fitness" of NGO demands with the prevailing episteme.

Contextual parameters

Chapter 2 maps the evolving political opportunities in the EU's external trade policymaking process. It assesses new access and participatory mechanisms established at the EU level to increase the participation of a broad base of non-state actors since the conclusion of the Uruguay Round. The chapter compares the changing role of NGOs in the EU's external trade policymaking process with other non-state actors, such as business associations and consumer advocates that have a vested interest in ongoing trade negotiations. It identifies remaining disparities in access encountered by economic and non-economic actors and it argues that improvements in the political opportunities for non-state actors reflect a robust democratic imperative in the EU. The chapter establishes a baseline from which to explore the conditions under which NGOs are empowered in trade politics and when their inclusion is likely to impact policy outcomes and make trade governance more legitimate.

A note on cases

The cases in this book were selected because they vary dramatically in the degree to which NGOs were formally involved in the EU's external trade policymaking process. Chapter 3 assesses the role of NGOs in a case that has been celebrated as indicative of the potential of global civil society to promote social justice and shape international public policy—the Access to Medicines campaign. Since the conclusion of the Uruguay Round of multilateral trade negotiations NGOs involved in the Access to Medicines campaign experienced sustained improvements in participatory and access conditions in the EU and are widely touted by EU policymakers as essential interlocutors in health-related trade negotiations. As such, this case should constitute an "easy test" for cosmopolitanism yet the findings tell a very different story.

Chapter 3 details the entrenchment of intellectual property rights (IPR) in the international trade regime and, by extension, the legal-liberal episteme. For the first time, stringent intellectual property norms were codified, legalized, and linked to the international trade regime. By situating IPR inside the legal-liberal episteme, WTO members defined, perhaps unconsciously, the "limits of the possible" in subsequent TRIPS negotiations. Chapter 3 shows that these ideational and legal constraints impacted and structured dialogue and consultation between NGOs and policymakers in the EU over the access to medicines issue. By tracing the role of NGOs in the formulation of the EU's position on TRIPS and access to medicines, the chapter shows that although NGOs have been instrumental in providing education, raising awareness, and giving a voice to broader societal concerns about the social and health-related aspects of proposed trade deals, they cannot determine policy outcomes in this arena. Contrary to conventional wisdom and the accounts of cosmopolitans, EU policymakers did not pursue policies that placed public health concerns over IPR protection, despite NGO involvement in the external trade policymaking process. Resisting co-optation, some NGOs have made the strategic choice to avoid engaging EU policymakers through formal channels of participation. Instead, they actively protest against the EU's external trade agenda from the streets and in the media. Chapter 4 explores this phenomenon by assessing the role of NGOs in shaping the EU's position on water services liberalization in the context of GATS negotiations.

With the creation of GATS, services were shifted out of the purview of national regulatory regimes to market-based rules in the international trade regime. Making commitments to liberalize services—such as water delivery, public health and education, and telecommunications—effectively entrenches those services within the legal-liberal episteme and locks in the range of possible future policy options. EU trade officials view "properly regulated" services liberalization, especially water services liberalization, as a win-win for sustainable development and EU offensive commercial interests. By contrast, many NGOs view services liberalization as an affront to democracy and human rights and, in response, launched an aggressive, multi-pronged campaign against the EU's pursuit of water services liberalization.

Chapter 4 situates the entrenchment of services in the legal-liberal episteme historically and assesses the major implications of this move. It then evaluates the impact of the NGO-led protest campaign against water services liberalization in the EU. Despite the dramatically different tactics, NGOs were effective in generating debate and awareness, educating the public, agenda setting, and giving a voice to broader societal concerns at the EU, national and municipal levels. However, as in the access to medicines case and despite support from some EU member states, members of the European Parliament and key players in the EU's water industry, NGOs were unable to bring about substantive and normative changes in policy. The robust legal-liberal episteme rendered NGO demands to drop the water services liberalization agenda incomprehensible to EU experts and technocrats.

At first it seemed as though NGOs had succeeded in influencing the EU's position, when it tempered its requests for third-country market access and then again when attention shifted to negotiating GATS commitments through plurilateral, collective requests, which do not address water for human use. However, the longer view shows that the EU remains committed to pursuing water services liberalization, particularly through GATS "Plus" agreements in PTAs, EPAs, and, possibly, through the newly proposed plurilateral Trade in Services Agreement (TiSA). The chapter argues that NGO efforts were effectively hamstrung by the legal-liberal episteme and that the EU has simply shifted forums to deflect, silence, and marginalize the NGO-led campaign.

Given that NGO agency is mediated and, often, constrained, by the social structure of global trade governance, the final chapter of the book reflects on the prospects for NGOs to bring about more meaningful change. It argues that the stakes are so high that tweaking at the margins of the dominant legal-liberal episteme is insufficient to deliver and safeguard public goods, make trade work for global development, and produce welfare gains for all, including the world's poorest people. Many cosmopolitans hang their hopes for a more just, equitable, and inclusive world on the involvement of NGOs in political processes. This chapter argues that we need to be more creative in thinking through the ways in which NGOs may challenge and fundamentally transform the epistemic foundations of global trade governance. While conventional advocacy has worked to give voice to broader societal concerns about trade, it has proven largely ineffectual in delivering substantive, normative change in policy. The book draws to a close by taking stock of the potential for NGOs to act as transformative actors, become knowledge producers, and open up alternative institutional pathways, modes of thinking, and spaces for resistance in global trade governance.

Notes

1 In 2009, the Treaty of Lisbon legally replaced the European Community (EC) and the three-pillar system—EC, Common Foreign and Security Policy, and Justice and Home Affairs—with a single, legally consolidated pillar, the European Union. For consistency, the book refers to the European Union, except when referring to specific treaty articles that predate the Treaty of Lisbon.

2 Annette Slob and Floor Smakman, "A Voice not a Vote: Evaluation of the Civil Society Dialogue at DG Trade," an independent review commissioned by the European Commission, Directorate-General for Trade (ECORYS Nederland BV, 2007), trade.ec.europa.eu/doclib/docs/2007/ma rch/tradoc_133527.pdf.

3 Max Weber, *Economy and Society: An Outline of Interpretive Sociology* (New York: Bedminster Press, 1968). Scharpf draws a similar distinction by arguing that legitimacy can either be won or lost on the input or output side of governance: Equality before the law, public consultation, and democratically elected officials are means to secure input legitimacy. Maximizing the efficiency and effectiveness of policy making via functional organizations and majoritarian decision-making are qualities leading to

output legitimacy. Though the distinction is analytically useful, it is unfortunate that Scharpf's (and many other scholars') usage of the term "output legitimacy" refers strictly to performance criteria such as efficiency and the problem-solving capacity of governments, rather than values such as fairness. Fritz Scharpf, *Governing in Europe: Effective and Democratic?* (Oxford: Oxford University Press, 1999).

4 See for example Margaret E. Keck and Kathryn Sikkink, *Activists Beyond Borders: Advocacy Networks in International Politics* (Ithaca, NY: Cornell University Press, 1998).

5 David Beetham and Christopher Lord, *Legitimacy and the European Union* (London: Longman, 1998); Markus Jachtenfuchs, Thomas Diez, and Sabine Jung, "Which Europe? Conflicting Models of a Legitimate European Political Order," *European Journal of International Relations* 4, no. 4 (1998): 409–445; Markus Höreth, "No Way Out for the Beast? The Unsolved Legitimacy Problem of European Governance," *Journal of European Public Policy* 6, no. 2 (1999): 249–268; Andrew Moravcsik, "Reassessing Legitimacy in the European Union," *Journal of Common Market Studies* 40, no. 4 (2002): 603–624; Christopher Lord, *A Democratic Audit of the European Union* (Basingstoke: Palgrave Macmillan, 2004); Andreas Føllesdal, "The Legitimacy Deficits of the European Union," *Journal of Political Philosophy* 14, no. 4 (2006): 441–468; Vivien A. Schmidt, *Democracy in Europe* (Oxford: Oxford University Press, 2006); and Simon Hix, *What's Wrong with the European Union and How to Fix It* (Cambridge: Polity Press, 2008).

6 Output legitimacy is at the core of utilitarian theories of legitimate rule emphasizing "government for the people," not "government by the people." See Robert Dahl and Edward Tuft, *Size and Democracy: The Politics of the Smaller European Democracies* (Stanford, Calif.: Stanford University Press, 1973); and Scharpf, *Governing in Europe*.

7 EU policies are legitimate to the extent that states have authorized EU-level decisions and any "autonomy of Union institutions is not evidence of their independent legitimacy, but of where it suits states to confer limited discretion on a supranational agent, according to a contract that is contingent, calculated and controlled": Christopher Lord and Paul Magnette, "E Pluribus Unum? Creative Disagreements about Legitimacy in the EU," *Journal of Common Market Studies* 42, no. 1 (2004): 185.

8 Giandomenico Majone, *Regulating Europe* (London: Routledge, 1996).

9 Even Majone now questions the quality and desirability of outputs generated by independent EU regulators. See Giandomenico Majone, *Dilemmas of European Integration* (Oxford: Oxford University Press, 2009).

10 Schmidt, *Democracy in Europe*.

11 Lars-Erik Cederman, "Nationalism and Bounded Integration: What Would it Take to Construct a European Demos?," *European Journal of International Relations* 7, no. 2 (2001): 249–275.

12 There are some notable exceptions. For instance, Scharpf, in *Governing in Europe: Effective and Democratic?*, denies that input legitimacy is possible at the EU level in the absence of an established demos.

13 Hix, *What's Wrong with the European Union and How to Fix It*.

14 Thomas Risse, *A Community of Europeans? Transnational Identities and Public Spheres* (Ithaca, NY: Cornell University Press, 2010); and Erik O.

Erikson, *Unfinished Democratization of Europe* (Oxford: Oxford University Press, 2009).

15 Judith Goldstein and Lisa Martin, "Legalization, Trade Liberalization and Domestic Politics: A Cautionary Note," *International Organization* 54, no. 3 (2000): 603–632.

16 John Boli and George M. Thomas, eds, *Constructing World Culture: International Non-Governmental Organizations since 1875* (Stanford, Calif.: Stanford University Press, 1999); Ann M. Florini, ed., *The Third Force: The Rise of Transnational Civil Society* (Washington, DC: Carnegie Endowment for International Peace, 2000); and Paul Wapner, "Politics Beyond the State: Environmental Activism and World Civic Politics," *World Politics* 47, no. 3 (1995): 311–340.

17 Robert O'Brien, Anne Marie Goertz, Jan Aart Scholte, and Marc Williams, *Contesting Global Governance: Multilateral Economic Institutions and Global Social Movements* (Cambridge: Cambridge University Press, 2000).

18 Anne Marie Clark, *Diplomacy of Conscience: Amnesty International and Changing Human Rights Norms* (Princeton, N.J.: Princeton University Press, 2001); Margaret E. Keck and Kathryn Sikkink, *Activists Beyond Borders: Advocacy Networks in International Politics* (Ithaca, NY: Cornell University Press, 1998); and Audie Klotz,*Norms in International Relations: The Struggle against Apartheid* (Ithaca, NY: Cornell University Press, 1995).

19 Thomas Risse-Kappen, Steve C. Ropp, and Kathryn Sikkink, eds, *The Power of Human Rights: International Norms and Domestic Change* (Cambridge: Cambridge University Press, 1999).

20 Elisabeth Corell and Michele M. Betsill, "NGO Influence in International Environmental Negotiations: A Framework for Analysis," *Global Environmental Politics* 1, no. 4 (2001): 65–85.

21 Richard Price, "Reversing the Gun Sights: Transnational Civil Society Targets Landmines," *International Organization* 52, no. 3 (1998): 613–644; and Kenneth R. Rutherford, "The Evolving Arms Control Agenda: Implications of the Role of NGOs in Banning Antipersonnel Landmines," *World Politics* 53, no. 1 (2000): 74–114.

22 Anne Marie Clark, Elisabeth J. Friedman, and Kathryn Hochstetler, "The Sovereign Limits of Global Civil Society: A Comparison of NGO Participation in UN World Conferences on the Environment, Human Rights and Women," *World Politics* 51, no. 1 (1998): 1–35.

23 Daniele Archibugi, *The Global Commonwealth of Citizens: Towards Cosmopolitan Democracy* (Princeton, N.J.: Princeton University Press, 2008); Daniele Archibugi and David Held, "Cosmopolitan Democracy: Paths and Agents," *Ethics and International Affairs* 25, no. 4 (2011): 433–461; and Magdalena Bexell, Johas Tahlberg, and Anders Uhlin, "Democracy in Global Governance: The Promises and Pitfalls of Transnational Actors," *Global Governance* 16, no. 1 (2010): 81–101.

24 Coined by Peter Gourevitch, "The Second Image Reversed: The International Sources of Domestic Politics," *International Organization* 32, no. 4 (1978): 881–912, this concept refers to the study of how developments at the international level impact domestic politics. Where NGOs are concerned, scholars tend to study how norm dissemination at the international

level motivates change in the domestic arena by way of the "boomerang effect" or the "spiral model." See respectively Keck and Sikkink, *Activists Beyond Borders: Advocacy Networks in International Politics*; and Risse, Ropp, and Sikkink, *The Power of Human Rights.*

25 See Erin Hannah, "The Quest for Accountable Governance: Embedded NGOs and Demand Driven Advocacy in the International Trade Regime," *Journal of World Trade* 48, no. 3 (2014): 460–461.

26 A notable exception is Silke Trommer, *Transformations in Trade Politics: Participatory Trade Politics in West Africa* (Abingdon: Routledge, 2014).

27 See for example, Daniel Drezner, *All Politics is Global: Explaining International Regulatory Regimes* (Princeton, N.J.: Princeton University Press, 2008), 21.

28 See Hannah Murphy, *The Making of International Trade Policy: NGOs, Agenda Setting and the WTO* (Northampton, Mass.: Edward Elgar, 2010).

29 David Armstrong, Valeria Bello, Julie Gilson, and Debora Spini, eds, *Civil Society and International Governance: The Role of Non-State Actors in the EU, Africa, Asia and Middle East* (Abingdon: Routledge, 2010); Jens Steffek, Claudia Kissling, and Patrizia Nanz, eds, *Civil Society Participation in European and Global Governance: A Cure for the Democratic Deficit?* (New York: Palgrave Macmillan, 2008); Jutta M. Joachim and Birgit Locher, *Transnational Activism in the UN and EU: A Comparative Study* (Abingdon: Routledge, 2008); Beate Kohler-Koch, "The Three Worlds of European Civil Society: What Role for Civil Society for What Kind of Europe?" *Policy and Society* 28, no. 1 (2009): 47–57; Ulrike Liebert and Hans-Jörg Trenz, eds, *The New Politics of European Civil Society* (Abingdon: Routledge, 2010); and Stijn Smismans and Nieves Pérez-Solórzano Borragán, "Europeanization, Third Sector and the Other Civil Society," *Journal of Civil Society* 6, no. 1 (2010): 77–82.

30 Christopher Ansell, Rahsaan Maxwell, and Daniela Sicurelli, "Protesting Food: NGOs and Political Mobilization in Europe," in *What's the Beef? The Contested Governance of European Food Safety*, ed. Christopher Ansell and David Vogel (Cambridge, Mass.: MIT Press, 2006), 97–122; G. Kristin Ronsendal, "Governing GMOs in the EU: A Deviant Case of Environmental Policy-making?" *Global Environmental Politics* 5, no. 1 (2005): 82–104.

31 Emek Uçarer, "Safeguarding Asylum as a Human Right: NGOs and the European Union," in *Transnational Activism in the UN and the EU*, ed. Jutta Joachim and Birgit Locher (New York: Routledge, 2009), 121–139.

32 Pauline Cullen, "Pan-European NGOs and Social Rights: Participatory Democracy and Civil Dialogue," in *Transnational Activism in the UN and the EU*, ed. Jutta Joachim and Birgit Locher (New York: Routledge, 2009), 134–146; and Pauline Cullen, "The Platform of European Social NGOs: Ideology, Division and Coalition," *Journal of Political Ideologies* 15, no. 3 (2010): 317–331.

33 Sophie Meunier, *Trading Voices: The European Union in International Commercial Negotiations* (Princeton, N.J.: Princeton University Press, 2005); and Andrea Ott, "EU Regulatory Agencies in EU External Relations: Trapped in a Legal Minefield Between European and International Law," *European Foreign Affairs Review* 13, no. 3 (2008): 515–540.

34 Steve Charnovitz, "The WTO and Cosmopolitics," *Journal of International Economic Law* 7, no. 3 (2004): 675–682; Baogang He and Hannah Murphy,

"Global Social Justice at the WTO? The Role of NGOs in Constructing Global Social Contracts," *International Affairs* 83, no. 4 (2007): 707–727; and Sylvia Ostry, "Dissent.com: How NGOs are Re-making the WTO," *Policy Options* 22, no. 5 (2001): 6–15.

35 Andreas Dür and Dirk De Bièvre, "Inclusion without Influence? NGOs in European Trade Policy," *Journal of Public Policy* 27, no. 1 (2007): 79–101.

36 Matthew Eagleton-Pearce, *Symbolic Power in the World Trade Organization* (Oxford: Oxford University Press, 2013).

37 Michel Foucault, *The Order of Things: An Archeology of the Human Sciences* (New York: Pantheon, 1970).

38 Emanuel Adler and Steven Bernstein, "Knowledge in Power: The Epistemic Construction of Global Governance," in *Power and Global Governance*, ed. Michael Barnett and Robert Duvall (Cambridge: Cambridge University Press, 2005).

1 Contesting cosmopolitan Europe

- The democratizing potential of NGOs in global governance
- NGOs, sustainable development, and welfare for all in global governance
- NGOs and the social structure of global governance
- Conclusion

Before we can begin to assess whether including NGOs results in more legitimate trade policymaking in the EU, we must first have a clear sense of what legitimacy means beyond the state. The aim of the first section of this chapter is to develop a post-national, principled conception of legitimacy based in the cosmopolitan international relations literature to serve as a benchmark for analysis. Legitimacy, in this view, can be assessed along procedural and substantive lines. Procedural legitimacy relates to democracy or "rule by the people"; governance can be legitimated when it rests on participation and control by affected people. The more opportunities for participation, open debate, rational reflection, and democratic empowerment are integrated into the governance system, the more legitimacy is attained. However, policy that entrenches asymmetrical power relations, unequal distribution of welfare gains, and runs roughshod over the environment cannot be considered legitimate, even if the process gives voice to affected people. In other words, post-national legitimacy means that policies are arrived at through democratic process and they promote and deliver the egalitarian distribution of global social goods.

Some scholars such as Bernstein claim that while it is clear that state consent is no longer an adequate basis for post-national legitimacy and there is a growing normative consensus that we need to democratize global governance, legitimacy criteria cannot be established *a priori*. Rather than devise a checklist or gold standard against which to assess the legitimacy of global governance institutions, Bernstein suggests that we should be mindful of the interaction between affected communities and social structures to identify evolving criteria of legitimacy that apply in different intergovernmental and non-state institutions, and across time.[1] I could not agree more that legitimacy is both contextually and historically contingent. However, the purpose here is not to offer a lengthy exposition on whether procedural legitimacy or cosmopolitan democracy is desirable, or to understand how these ideas came to constitute received wisdom. Rather, the purpose of this discussion is to unpack cosmopolitan assumptions about what should happen if we add more NGOs to global governance and stir.

Progressive NGOs are widely conceived as agents of cosmopolitan democracy and social justice, representing global citizens' needs and concerns, and capable of giving voice to otherwise marginalized people. Including NGOs is thought likely to lead to more participatory, accountable, transparent, progressive, and socially just global governance.[2] Indeed, for Scholte, NGO "involvement could inject values and voice that bolster the moral and democratic legitimacy of global governance."[3] However, a few cautionary notes are in order because NGOs are not themselves inherently legitimating.

First, we must be aware that not all NGOs are progressive and some may even pursue ends that are racist, hateful, unethical, or violent. This book is most concerned with the inclusion of NGOs that claim to be socially progressive and that seek to re-embed global markets in broader social and environmental values, and that are working to give a voice to poor countries in an effort to correct imbalances and asymmetries in the international trade regime. However, the ends they pursue are not uncontested or intrinsically good; rather, the inputs they generate need to be critically examined.

Second, we must be mindful of the geographical attributes of NGOs. Many of those involved in the EU's external trade policymaking process are, for example, based in the global North and are directed by Western-educated, middle-class people who speak from a position of privilege.[4] This raises questions about the appropriateness of NGOs claiming to give voice to the poor and marginalized in international trade negotiations, and raises the risk that NGOs may serve to reproduce social hierarchies or inequalities in the global economy.[5]

Third, there are concerns about the internal accountability of NGOs and whether they have sufficient transparency, representativeness, and participatory mechanisms to ensure their own internal accountability.[6] Critics also raise questions about the external accountability of NGOs—to whom are they accountable and by what mechanisms?[7] We must be on the lookout for weak democratic credentials of NGOs and be sure to assess the quality as well as the quantity of the inputs they generate. These questions also point to the fact that including NGOs in the policymaking process is certainly not sufficient for legitimating governance and may even serve to delegitimize it where they expose malfeasance by global authorities.[8] Rather, the inclusion of NGOs is but one mechanism by which to subject the attainment, exercise, and distribution of power in global governance to scrutiny.

The second section of this chapter argues that cosmopolitans pay insufficient attention to the social structure of global governance. We must consider how NGO claims to democracy and the egalitarian distribution of global social goods are mediated by the ideational and normative parameters of decision-making. Epistemes, not formal inclusion or exclusion in the policymaking process, structure patterns of empowerment and enable and delimit NGO agency in global governance, and in the EU's external trade policymaking process in particular. While cosmopolitan and constructivist accounts both anticipate improvements in procedural legitimacy to follow from the inclusion of NGOs in policymaking, they tell very different stories about the mechanisms at work and the substance of policy outputs. The aim of this chapter is to unpack these stories.

The democratizing potential of NGOs in global governance

The dis-embedding of social, political, and economic relations from the state are key features of contemporary global governance, best defined as "the sum of the informal and formal ideas, values, norms, procedures, and institutions that help all actors—states, IGOs [intergovernmental organizations], civil society, and [M]NCs [multinational corporations]—identify, understand, and address trans-boundary problems."[9] There is a growing recognition that the most pressing global problems—alleviating poverty, mitigating environmental degradation, and respecting planetary boundaries, stemming pandemics and terrorism, and addressing social goals including basic human rights, employment, gender equality, health, education, and other necessary requirements of a decent quality of life—are beyond the capacity of individual states to resolve and require global solutions. Though undeniably inadequate in its current form,[10] we have an emerging web of global governance without global government, a multitude of cooperative problem-solving arrangements at different levels (whether formal or informal, permanent or temporary, state-based, non-state, networks, or partnerships) that aim to plug the gaps created by states' inability or unwillingness to address global problems.[11] The locus of political authority is increasingly complex, diffuse, and dynamic as competency and decision-making are shifted upwards to supranational organizations such as the EU and downwards to local or regional authorities that often bypass national governments. Non-state and public-private partnerships are working alongside public authorities to manage global problems and altogether new forms of governance, where authority rests primarily in the market, are becoming more prevalent day by day.[12] These developments in global governance are in deep tension with democracy and social justice.

Democracy minimally requires that affected persons have equivalent opportunities to participate in and exercise control over the exercise of power. Within the state, democratic governance "rests minimally on consent of the people governed or popular sovereignty, and, increasingly, on democratic process and participation, accountability, and some basic political and citizenship rights."[13] The fragmentation and decentralization of political authority in global governance has created a so-called democratic deficit because it has not been matched by equivalent democratic mechanisms beyond the state. For cosmopolitan scholars such as Scholte, while procedural democracy is the dominant principle legitimating political authority,[14] "contemporary global spaces are not democratic spaces. Global governance is not democratically legitimate. We do not have a situation where the governed have accorded the right of rule to existing regimes."[15] Democratic mechanisms largely remain nested inside the state even as increasingly sensitive decisions regarding the world's most pressing problems are taken up at regional and global levels. Cosmopolitans contend that global democracy cannot begin and end with the state, and have set an agenda for creating mechanisms at the global, regional, national, and local levels to increase democratic control of global governance.[16]

Some critics contend that the democratic deficit in global governance is illusionary because decision-making authority originates from and is authorized by the popular authority of member states to international organizations.[17] While the accountability and transparency of international organizations could be improved, as long as the democratic credentials of states are in order, democracy beyond the state is not a problem.[18] As noted in the introduction, Majone offers perhaps the boldest statement along these lines, claiming that democratic controls would actually interfere with the good performance of institutions such as the European Commission.[19] In their public standard for assessing the legitimacy of global governance institutions, Buchanan and Keohane offer a more nuanced view by denying the sufficiency of state consent and arguing that global governance must be consonant with democratic values. Nonetheless, they dismiss claims to global democracy as naïve and infeasible.[20]

Others contend that the whole notion of global democracy is an oxymoron since democracy is a form of governance under which the power to govern lies with the people, the *demos*.[21] Democracy requires a community of people who share a collective identity, sentiment, solidarity, and a degree of social cohesion; the legitimacy of the political order is thought to depend on the existence of social homogeneity between its members.[22] A global demos is thus inconceivable, both conceptually and empirically, beyond the state. Instead, the autonomy of clearly demarcated, territorially based political communities must be protected by an exclusive and minimal allocation of competencies to global governance institutions.[23] Some go farther to suggest that a *demos* can only really be established at the local level. A process of "de-globalization" or the stripping down of global governance, therefore, would best serve democracy.[24]

For cosmopolitans, the statist critique simply does not match up with structures of authority in global governance or the transborder character of the most pressing global problems.[25] In Scholte's view, "if deepened global relations are here to stay for the foreseeable future, a conclusion that global democracy is untenable would surrender the field to global oligarchy. Such an outcome—which contradicts most notions of a good society—must be resisted."[26] In this vein, it no longer makes sense to talk about autonomous, homogenous, or exclusive, territorially bounded political communities. Indeed, it is doubtful if it ever really made sense if we take seriously Murphy's claim that we have had some form of global governance since at least the nineteenth century.[27] Who constitutes "the people" is increasingly fluid as "'overlapping communities of fate'; that is, a state of affairs in which the fortune and prospects of individual political communities are increasingly bound together" multiply.[28] By appealing to the "all-affected principle," the idea that all those affected by a political decision should have a say in its making, cosmopolitans have effectively loosened the boundaries between the state and democracy.[29]

The most compelling cosmopolitan treatments of political community understand that individuals have multiple solidarities—to humankind, to multiple nations, to the region, and to non-territorial affinities such as religion, gender, and race.[30] Rather than aspire to the construction of a single, global *demos*, Bohman, for example, argues that global democracy should be promoted horizontally through the development of plural and overlapping "demoi" at local, regional, and global levels.[31] Still in the embryonic stages, demoi can be promoted through the construction of democratic and deliberative spaces where opportunities for participation, political debate, collective deliberation, and direct engagement with decision-makers may catalyze feelings of solidarity and the development of a new public sphere.[32] It is here that we can locate the cosmopolitan promise of NGOs for improving the procedural legitimacy of global governance.

Indeed, it is possible to delineate at least five complementary ways through which NGOs can promote "rule by the people" and improve the procedural legitimacy of the EU's external trade policymaking process specifically.[33] First, NGOs may engage in public education activities, disseminating information and generating public awareness of key trade-related issues. Fostering knowledgeable or informed citizens who can involve themselves meaningfully in governance is key to democracy and public officials may facilitate the transfer of ideas and information between NGOs and citizens of the EU. Second, NGOs can stimulate and improve the quality of public debate and deliberation about substantive policy issues, normative ideas about the egalitarian distribution of social goods, and about the democratic quality of governance itself. Their involvement in governance can serve to widen policy debates and accommodate the expression of multiple and critical views, even when they challenge prevailing policy orthodoxy. Third, NGOs can give voice and recognition to otherwise marginalized groups that have been silenced by policymaking beyond the state and/ or by arbitrary social hierarchies. Fourth, policymaking is likely to become more transparent and open to public scrutiny as NGOs push for access to documents, make information about the substance of trade negotiations more widely available, and monitor, scrutinize, and assess the development and impact of trade policy. Finally, NGOs may play a watchdog function, improving the public accountability and responsiveness of decision-makers by publicizing grievances or naming and shaming in the media.

NGOs, sustainable development, and welfare for all in global governance

It is simply not enough, however, to improve the democratic credentials of global governance. There is no guarantee that adding more NGOs and stirring will correct policies that entrench asymmetrical power relations, destroy the environment, and exacerbate the precarity of the world's poorest people by promoting the inequitable distribution of global social goods. The objective is not "to achieve hegemonic legitimacy in a Gramscian sense, where the subjects of global governance are persuaded that the rules operate in their interest when the regime in fact oppresses them."[34] We must also interrogate the projected outcomes and consequences of policy to fully understand the significance of giving a voice to NGOs in policymaking. Although there are many variants, cosmopolitan notions of post-national substantive legitimacy are anchored to an awareness of individuals' equal moral worth, a global consciousness, and the belief that justice should not be the sole responsibility of the state in a globalizing world. Under contemporary conditions, human lives are increasingly played out in the world as a single place—the life chances of individuals in developed, developing and least developed countries are interdependent and we therefore have obligations to one another. At a minimum, post-national substantive legitimacy requires an awareness of these changes and a concern for how our actions respond to and shape what is occurring elsewhere in the world. As Pogge argues:

> [w]e must reflect upon social institutions and the roles and offices that they involve as one [global] scheme, against the background of feasible alternative schemes. This reflection is highly abstract, but without it we cannot even begin to understand what we are doing to others, how we are involved in their lives, and what concrete responsibilities we might have towards them.[35]

Among cosmopolitan IR scholars, Pogge and Beitz provide the most insight for thinking through the potential role of NGOs because their theories of global distributive justice center on the reform of global governance institutions. They part company with those cosmopolitans for whom principles of distributive justice apply to all on the basis of the equal moral status of human beings.[36] Instead, they understand individuals to be members of multiple, overlapping, morally relevant communities and advance consequence-based theories of global distributive justice that apply to individuals whose life chances and prospects are affected by a common institutional structure.[37] Principles of distributive justice should be applied based on the extensity of social relations and the impact of the global "rules of the game."[38] Advancing the "all-affected principle," Beitz claims "the requirements of justice apply to institutions and practices ... in which social activity produces relative and absolute benefits and burdens that would not exist if the social activity did not take place."[39] Advocating for the global application of Rawls's difference principle,[40] Pogge "asserts the fundamental negative duty of justice as one that every human being owes to every other ... We have a negative duty not to impose an unjust institutional order upon any human beings—compatriots or foreigners."[41] Rather, international rules and institutions should be reorganized to achieve a more just distribution of benefits and burdens, and to ensure that the welfare of the globally least advantaged people are maximized.[42]

For Pogge, the world's poorest people are actively being harmed by an unjust system of international institutions designed for and by the rich.[43] Nowhere is this more in evidence than the multilateral trading system. In his account of the WTO, Wilkinson paints a chilling picture of a profoundly iniquitous system that has entrenched asymmetries more deeply with each round of negotiations and failed to produce development for all. Despite rhetorical claims to the contrary, the lives of the least advantaged have become more precarious as the vast majority of welfare gains accrue to industrialized countries.[44] The question is whether the inclusion of progressive NGOs in trade governance can help redress this unsustainable state of affairs.

In particular, if the inclusion of progressive NGOs improves the substantive legitimacy of the EU's external trade policymaking process we should see policy outputs resulting from their participation along the following lines. First, policymakers should pursue trade policies that aim to balance the three pillars of sustainable development and respond to social and environmental concerns, not just economic demands. Second, they should aim to redress unfair terms of trade and pursue policies aimed at the more equitable global distribution of welfare gains from trade, such that poor countries benefit most. Third, they should pursue policies aimed at redistributing the burdens associated with international trade from the global South to the global North such that poor countries have sufficient policy space and flexibility to pursue other social goals necessary for a decent quality of life.

NGOs and the social structure of global governance

With all the caveats noted above in mind, cosmopolitans hold a very optimistic view of the potential for NGOs to improve the post-national legitimacy of global governance, and the EU's external trade policymaking process in particular. It is the central contention of this section that these hopes are exaggerated because they do not adequately account for the ideational and normative constraints of global governance. If we take these things seriously, we see that the role of NGOs is more promissory than actual, despite improvements in participation and access. Epistemes, not formal inclusion or exclusion in policymaking, determines who has a voice in global trade.

Beginning with John Ruggie, the episteme concept has gained currency in IR scholarship.[45] Indeed, the "epistemic communities" literature has generated a small cottage industry focused on the epistemic dimension of world politics.[46] Generally speaking, this body of scholarship views epistemes as "the attribute of science-based agents ... who seek to socially construct policy in their image of the truth and principled beliefs" in order to promote international cooperation.[47]

The framework offered here builds upon a much broader conceptualization of episteme based in Foucault's work,[48] adapted to IR and made amenable to empirical research by Adler and Bernstein.[49] Accordingly, epistemes are the building blocks of global governance. They comprise shared, intersubjective or taken-for-granted causal and evaluative assumptions about how the world works. They are invisible lenses that allow human beings to interpret and make sense of the world; people are rarely conscious of the fundamental assumptions that comprise the episteme except at critical junctures.[50] They are so powerful precisely because they are generally taken for granted. Essentially, epistemes help people categorize, simplify, and systematize what they experience in the world.

Epistemes are not reducible to strategic or material interests because they are embedded in institutions and in common discourse through which people communicate about the world and define the range of problems that can be addressed. For Adler and Bernstein, "[e]pisteme thus refers to the 'bubble' within which people happen to live, the way people construe their reality, their basic understandings of the causes of things, their normative beliefs, and their identity, the understanding of self in terms of others."[51] Notably, epistemes are numerous and permeable; the predominant episteme is just one among several possible sets of lenses through which to view the world.

Epistemes are powerful because they dispose human beings to behave in particular ways and they delineate the limits of the possible; they contain "background knowledge" or boundaries within which people reason and make choices. These boundaries may consist of "widely held accepted norms, consensual scientific knowledge, ideological beliefs deeply accepted by the collective, and so on."[52] Essentially, epistemes structure which actions and practices are conceivable and which are unimaginable. The shift from GATT to WTO, in particular, served to institutionalize or further entrench a hybrid legal-liberal episteme in the international trade regime, and this has implications for external trade policy governance in the EU.

The liberal aspects of the episteme are well known, and its tenets are beyond reproach in the international trade regime. At its core is a philosophy about the market and the belief that open markets and free trade are panaceas for development and economic growth. The shift from GATT to WTO dramatically extended trade rules into services, investment, and intellectual property rights, and the scope of trade rules has expanded well beyond managing barriers to trade at the border to shaping national labour, environmental, human health, food safety, and development policies. Although policy prescriptions in the international trade regime have varied over time, "they only reflected 'political compromises' ... to the degree they create the necessary stability to further the goals of liberalization."[53]

The shift from GATT to WTO also shifted power to the legal (as opposed to the political). The WTO Agreements are judicially protected by the WTO's robust DSU which prevents deviation from liberal market principles and insulates the free functioning of the market from political interference. The imposition of international legal constraints on governments is intended to make commitments more credible and transparent. Compliance with the rule of law "identifies acceptable versus unacceptable forms of governance, privileges a particular kind of knowledge and discourse (legal-rational), and defines insiders and outsiders—those who follow the 'rule of law' and those who do not."[54] Legal constraints also ensure fair and consistent application of the rules and make the business environment for traders and investors more stable and predictable. Finally, legal constraints work to disembed market transactions from public scrutiny and social and environmental regulation. Legalization in the WTO is, in essence, the rule of law counterpart to the liberal or free market episteme. It serves to institutionalize rules that entrench rights for investors and corporations and serves as the focal point for resistance and growing demands by NGOs for a voice in trade policymaking.

Finally, epistemes provide people with a social identity, a political language, a political agenda, and standards of political action. They empower technocrats and experts relative to other actors, including NGOs and firms or business associations; as the episteme gains resonance and legalization extends into more complex and technical areas of international trade, these actors gain power. Their work serves to maintain and reinforce dominant and largely universal norms, intersubjective ideas, rules of appropriate behavior, consensual scientific knowledge, and ideological beliefs. Experts and technocrats gain functional authority relative to non-state actors where they are required to make authoritative interpretations of the rules; where they are required to develop standards in technical areas; or, through specialized cause-effect knowledge, where their (policy) prescriptions gain legitimacy as focal points for cooperation, or the basis for new rules.[55] Moreover, experts and technocrats are themselves the product of the dominant episteme, and they work to co-opt and absorb forces of global civil society that resist or reject the prevailing episteme. Those who cannot be co-opted, who reject the episteme wholesale, and who operate on the margins of the governing arrangement will be cast as outsiders and their work will be actively de-legitimized by policymakers.

Conclusion

The following chapters show that EU policymakers responded positively to NGO demands for a voice and a role in external trade policymaking. In an effort to reproduce and legitimize the legal-liberal episteme, steps were taken to make policymaking more transparent, accountable and open to participation by a wider range of non-state actors. New opportunities for access and participation enabled those that accept the main tenets of the legal-liberal episteme to serve as interlocutors in the policymaking process; where discussions concerned the broad trajectory of policy, these actors played the role of educators and agenda setters. NGOs that contested the episteme and operated on the margins of the governance arrangement also improved the procedural legitimacy of policymaking by giving voice to broader societal concerns, and generating public debate and awareness.

Where policy discussions concerned the nuts and bolts of trade agreements or highly technical aspects of trade negotiations, policymakers pulled away from broadly participatory processes and actively sought to delegitimize the work of those who challenged the dominant episteme, leading to a retrenchment of procedural legitimacy. Because technocrats and experts possess an authoritative claim on knowledge, the more technical (as opposed to political) the issue, the more functional power will pool in their hands. Political compromises with NGOs were only struck when they were necessary to further the core goals of the episteme. This pattern of empowerment precluded the possibility of introducing the policies advanced by NGOs because they were inconsistent with the requirements of the prevailing episteme and, therefore, largely incomprehensible as policy solutions to decision-makers. Indeed, NGOs that could not be co-opted were de-legitimized and silenced. The cases in Chapters 3 and 4 show that, on balance, NGOs improved the procedural legitimacy of external trade policymaking both from inside and outside formal participatory channels. However, the prevailing episteme hamstrung their efforts to bring about trade policies that would promote sustainable development, prioritize public health, and deliver welfare gains for all.

Notes

1 Steven Bernstein, "Legitimacy in Intergovernmental and Non-State Global Governance," *Review of International Political Economy* 18, no. 1 (2011): 17–51.
2 Thomas Risse, "Transnational Actors and World Politics," in *Handbook of International Relations*, ed. W. Carlsnaes, T. Risse, and B. Simmons (London: Sage, 2001).
3 Jan Aart Scholte, "Civil Society and the Legitimation of Global Governance," *Journal of Civil Society* 3, no. 3 (2007): 305.
4 Jens Steffek and Patrizia Nanz, "Emergent Patterns of Civil Society Participation in Global and European Governance," in *Civil Society Participation in European and Global Governance: A Cure for the Democratic Deficit?*, ed. Jens Steffek, Claudia Kissling, and Patrizia Nanz (Basingstoke: Palgrave Macmillan, 2008).
5 Tanja Brühl, "Representing the People? NGOs in International Negotiations," in *Evaluating Transnational NGOs: Legitimacy, Accountability, Representation*, ed. Jens Steffek and Kristina Hahn (Basingstoke: Palgrave Macmillan, 2010); and Bernard Beauzamy, "Transnational Social Movements and Democratic Legitimacy," in *Legitimacy Beyond the State?: Reexamining the Democratic Credentials of Transnational Actors*, ed. Eva Erman and Anders Uhlin (Basingstoke: Palgrave Macmillan, 2010)
6 Martina Piewitt, Meike Rodekamp, and Jens Steffek, "Civil Society in World Politics: How Accountable are Transnational CSOs?," *Journal of Civil Society* 6, no. 3 (2010): 237–258.
7 Jonas Tallberg and Anders Uhlin, "Civil Society and Global Democracy: An Assessment," in *Global Democracy: Normative and Empirical Assessments*, ed. Daniele Archibugi, Mathias Koenig-Archibugi, and Raffaele Marchetti (Cambridge: Cambridge University Press, 2011).
8 Scholte, "Civil Society and the Legitimation of Global Governance," 310.
9 Thomas G. Weiss and Rorden Wilkinson, "Rethinking Global Governance? Complexity, Authority, Power, Change," *International Studies Quarterly* 58, no. 1 (2014): 211. See also Jan Aart Scholte, "Reinventing Global Democracy," *European Journal of International Relations* 20, no. 1 (2014): 3–28; and Michael Barnett and Martha Finnemore, *Rules for the World* (Ithaca, NY: Cornell University Press, 2004).
10 Thomas G. Weiss, *Global Governance: Why? What? Whither?* (Cambridge: Polity Press, 2013).
11 A term first coined by James Rosenau and Ernet-Otto Czempel, eds, *Governance without Government: Order and Change in World Politics* (Cambridge: Cambridge University Press, 1992).
12 For one of the most insightful statements on thinking through the past, present, and future of global governance to date, see Weiss and Wilkinson, "Rethinking Global Governance?," 207–215.
13 Steven Bernstein, "The Elusive Basis of Legitimacy in Global Governance: Three Conceptions," *Globalization and Autonomy Working Paper Series* GHC04/2 (2004): 6.
14 For David Held, *Democracy and the Global Order: From the Modern State to Cosmopolitan Governance* (Stanford, Calif.: Stanford University Press, 1995), 1: "Democracy bestows an aura of legitimacy on modern political life: laws, rules, and policies appear justified when they are democratic."

15 Jan Aart Scholte, "Civil Society and Democracy in Global Governance," *Global Governance* 8, no. 3 (2002): 292.

16 Daniele Archibugi and David Held, "Cosmopolitan Democracy: Paths and Agents," *Ethics and International Affairs* 25, no. 4 (2011): 433–461.

17 Andrew Moravcsik, "Is There a 'Democratic Deficit' in World Politics? A Framework for Analysis," *Government and Opposition* 39, no. 2 (2004): 336–363; Robert Dahl, "Can International Institutions be Democratic? A Skeptic's View," in *Democracy's Edges*, ed. Ian Shapiro and Casiano Hacker-Cordon (Cambridge: Cambridge University Press, 1999), 19–36.

18 Robert O. Keohane and Andrew Moravcsik, "Democracy-Enhancing Multilateralism," *International Organization* 63, no. 1 (2009): 1–31.

19 Giandomenico Majone, *Regulating Europe* (Abingdon: Routledge, 1996).

20 Allen Buchanan and Robert O. Keohane, "The Legitimacy of Global Governance Institutions," *Ethics & International Affairs* 20, no. 4 (2006): 405–437.

21 Dahl, "Can International Institutions be Democratic? A Skeptic's View," 19–26; and Jaap de Wilde, "The Mirage of Global Democracy," *European Review* 19, no. 1 (2011): 5–18. For a critical discussion see Mathias Koenig-Archibugi, "Is Global Democracy Possible?" *European Journal of International Relations* 17, no. 3 (2011): 519–542; Christina List and Mathias Koenig-Archibugi, "Can there be a Global Demos? An Agency-Based Approach," *Philosophy and Public Affairs* 38, no. 1 (2010): 76–110; and Daniel Archibugi, "Cosmopolitan Democracy and its Critics: A Review," *European Journal of International Relations* 10, no. 3 (2004): 437–473.

22 Brigid Laffan, "The Politics of Identity and Political Order in Europe," *Journal of Common Market Studies* 34, no. 1 (1996): 81–102.

23 Will Kymlicka, *Politics in the Vernacular: Nationalism, Multiculturalism and Citizenship* (Oxford: Oxford University Press, 2000); Craig Calhoun, *Nations Matter: Culture, History, and the Cosmopolitan Dream* (New York: Routledge, 2007); and Terry Macdonald, "Boundaries Beyond Borders: Delineating Democratic 'Peoples' in a Globalizing World," *Democratization* 10, no. 3 (2003): 173–194.

24 Scholte, "Reinventing Global Democracy," 12; Walden Bello, *Deglobalization: Ideas for a New Global Economy* (London: Zed Books, 2005); and Gianpaolo Baiocchi, *Militants and Citizens: The Politics of Participatory Democracy in Porto Alegre* (Redwood City, Calif.: Stanford University Press, 2005). See also Teivo Teivainen and Heikki Patomäki, *A Possible World: Democratic Transformations of Global Institutions* (London and New York: Zed Books, 2004).

25 For a robust rebuttal of the statist critique see Scholte, "Reinventing Global Democracy," 3–28; and Archibugi, "Cosmopolitan Democracy and its Critics: A Review," 437–473. See also John Markoff, "Democracy's Past Transformations, Present Challenges, and Future Prospects," *International Journal of Sociology* 43, no. 2 (2013): 13–40.

26 Scholte, "Reinventing Global Democracy," 12.

27 Craig Murphy, "Global Governance over the Long Haul," *International Studies Quarterly* 58, no. 1 (2014): 216–218; and Craig Murphy, *International Organization and Industrial Change: Global Governance Since 1850* (Cambridge: Polity Press 1994).

28 David Held and Anthony McGrew, "The End of the Old Order? Globalization and the Prospects for World Order," *Review of International Studies* 24, no. 5 (1998): 237.

29 Jürgen Habermas, *Post-National Constellation: Political Essays* (Cambridge, Mass.: Massachusetts Institute for Technology Press, 2001); and Andrew Linklater, *The Transformation of Political Community* (Cambridge: Polity Press, 1998). On the all-affected principle see Sofia Näsström, "The Challenge of the All-Affected Principle," *Political Studies* 59, no. 1 (2011): 116–134.

30 Scholte, "Reinventing Global Democracy," 14; Held, *Democracy and the Global Order.*

31 James Bohman, "From Demos to Demoi: Democracy across Borders," *Ratio Juris* 18, no. 2 (2005): 293–314.

32 Jürgen Habermas, *Between Facts and Norms: Contributions to a Discourse Theory of Democracy and Law* (Cambridge, Mass.: Massachusetts Institute of Technology Press, 1992); John Dryzek, *Deliberative Global Politics* (Cambridge: Polity Press, 2006); and John Dryzek, *Foundations and Frontiers of Deliberative Governance* (Oxford: Oxford University Press, 2010).

33 This section builds on the insights of Jan Aart Scholte, the leading cosmopolitan authority on the role of civil society in global governance. See, in particular, Jan Aart Scholte, ed., *Building Global Democracy: Civil Society and Accountable Global Governance* (Cambridge: Cambridge University Press, 2011); Jan Aart Scholte, "A More Inclusive Global Governance? The IMF and Civil Society in Africa," *Global Governance* 18, no. 2 (2012): 185–206; and Scholte, "Civil Society and the Legitimation of Global Governance," 305–326.

34 Scholte, "Civil Society and the Legitimation of Global Governance," 311.

35 Thomas Pogge, *Realizing Rawls* (Ithaca, NY: Cornell University Press, 1989), 9.

36 Peter Singer, "Famine, Affluence, and Morality," *Philosophy and Public Affairs* 1, no. 1 (1972): 229–243; Peter Singer, *One World: The Ethics of Globalization* (New Haven, Conn.: Yale University Press, 2002); and Peter Unger, *Living High and Letting Die: Our Illusion of Innocence* (Oxford: Oxford University Press, 1996).

37 The idea that the scope of distributive justice is coextensive with the impact of rules and institutions departs significantly from Rawls's understanding of distributive justice as fair reciprocity. For Rawls, principles of distributive justice apply only to those who contributed to the creation of certain benefits. See John Rawls, *A Theory of Justice* (Cambridge, Mass.: Harvard University Press, 1971), 342–343. Pogge and Beitz aim to correct the exclusivity of Rawls's theory by placing emphasis on the degree to which individuals are affected by institutional rules and norms.

38 Pogge, *Realizing Rawls*, 274.

39 Charles Beitz, *Political Theory and International Relations* (Princeton, N.J.: Princeton University Press, 1979), 131.

40 As Bernstein notes in "The Elusive Basis of Legitimacy in Global Governance," 18, "Rawls explicitly rejects its international application in both *Theory* and *Law of Peoples*, instead arguing only for "a duty to assist other peoples living under unfavourable conditions that prevent them from having a just or decent political social regime." Indeed, for Rawls, *A Theory of Justice*, 114–118 and 333–342, natural duties are the only

international moral requirements. However, Pogge, *Realizing Rawls*, 276, argues obligations of global distributive justice arise because "a global institutional scheme is imposed by all of us on each of us."

41 Thomas Pogge, "Cosmopolitanism: A Defense," *Critical Review of International Social and Political Philosophy* 5, no. 3 (2002): 89; and Thomas Pogge, "'Assisting' the Global Poor," in *Global Ethics: Seminal Essays*, ed. Thomas Pogge and Keith Horton (St Paul, Minn.: Paragon House, 2008), 531–564.

42 Thomas Pogge, "Rawls and Global Justice," *The Canadian Journal of Philosophy* 18, no. 2 (1988): 233; Beitz, *Political Theory and International Relations*, 52.

43 Thomas Pogge, *World Poverty and Human Rights*, second edition (Cambridge: Polity Press, 2008).

44 Rorden Wilkinson, *What's Wrong with the WTO and How to Fix It* (Cambridge: Polity Press, 2014).

45 John Gerard Ruggie, "International Responses to Technology: Concepts and Trends," *International Organization* 29, no. 3 (1975): 557–583.

46 Emanuel Adler, "The Emergence of Cooperation: National Epistemic Communities and the International Evolution of the Idea of Nuclear Arms Control," *International Organization* 46, no. 1 (1992): 101–45; Emanuel Adler, "Seeds of Peaceful Change: The OSCE's Security Community-building Model," in *Security Communities*, ed. Emanuel Adler and Michael Barnett (New York: Cambridge University Press, 1998), 119–159; Peter M. Haas, ed., "Power, Knowledge, and International Policy Coordination," *International Organization* Special Issue 46, no. 1 (1992); Martha Finnemore, "International Organizations as Teachers of Norms: The United Nations Educational, Scientific, and Cultural Organization and Science Policy," *International Organization* 47, no. 4 (1993): 565–597; Martha Finnemore, *National Interests in International Society* (Ithaca, NY: Cornell University Press, 1996); Jeffrey W. Legro, "Whence American Internationalism," *International Organization* 52, no. 4 (2000): 253–289; and John Gerard Ruggie, "Territoriality and Beyond: Problematizing Modernity in International Relations," *International Organization* 47, no. 1 (1993): 139–174.

47 Emanuel Adler and Steven Bernstein, "Knowledge in Power: The Epistemic Construction of Global Governance," in *Power and Global Governance*, ed. Michael Barnett and Raymond Duvall (Cambridge: Cambridge University Press, 2005), 295.

48 Michel Foucault, *The Order of Things: An Archeology of the Human Sciences* (New York: Pantheon, 1970).

49 Adler and Bernstein, "Knowledge in Power," 294–318.

50 Markus Kornprobst, "Argumentation and Compromise: Ireland's Selection of the Territorial Status Quo Norm," *International Organization* 61, no. 1 (2007): 69–98.

51 Adler and Bernstein, "Knowledge in Power," 296.

52 Ibid., 303.

53 Ibid., 312.

54 Ibid., 310.

55 Ibid., 304.

2 The evolution of EU trade politics
Agency, competency, and decision-making processes

- **The trade-related competency of the EU**
- **Institutional dynamics in EU external trade governance**
- **Political opportunities and non-state actors in EU trade politics**
- **Conclusion**

In the years following the WTO's so-called Battle of Seattle, the European Union introduced a number of measures aimed at giving voice to a wide range of non-state actors in the external trade policymaking process. EU policymakers realized that they would ignore critics of trade at their peril and therefore sought to formalize political opportunities for both economic and non-economic non-state actors to communicate their trade-related concerns to the European Commission and, to a lesser extent, the European Parliament (EP). These improvements in the EU's political opportunity structure took place alongside a widening of trade competency and shifting institutional dynamics in the external trade decision-making process. Taken together, these changes reflect a robust, cosmopolitan, democratic imperative in the EU that undoubtedly improved the input legitimacy of EU trade politics, particularly along the lines of public deliberation, transparency, inclusivity, and accountability.

This chapter seeks to map these changes in order to establish the wider context within which NGOs sought to influence the EU's position at the WTO on access to medicines and water services liberalization. Part one details the evolution of external trade governance in the EU.[1] A two-tier delegation of authority has historically characterized external trade policymaking and the analysis situates non-state actors at the second level (day-to-day negotiations). The ongoing controversy over competency is also discussed in order to show that, like its industrial country counterparts, the EU functions largely according to a fiduciary logic of delegation. The changing balance of power between the EU institutions is potentially the most significant change, particularly since the Treaty of Lisbon (ToL) entered into force in 2009. The increased competency of the EU coupled with an enhanced role for the EP has improved the accountability, transparency, and opportunities for participation by non-state actors in external trade policymaking.

Part two traces the role of non-state actors in the EU's external trade policymaking process since the creation of the WTO in 1995. It examines the changing political opportunity structure by looking at access and participatory conditions in the major EU institutions—the Council of the EU, the EP, and the European Commission. Particular attention is given to the formal, consultative processes in Directorate-General (DG) Trade. On balance, improvements in participatory opportunities have been significant and are unparalleled elsewhere across industrialized countries. However, disparities in access and participation between economic and non-economic actors persist, especially in DG Trade.

The trade-related competency of the EU

External trade has always been one of the most deeply integrated policy areas in the EU, second only to the internal market. The Treaty of Rome called for an internal market with no obstacles to trade and strong competition, as well as for multilateral liberalization. The first major step towards internal liberalization was achieved with the Customs Union formed in 1968. This cornerstone of EU trade policy explicitly pursues the following:

1   free circulation of goods originating in the EC member states;
2   adoption of a common customs tariff and Common Commercial Policy (CCP); and
3   as a consequence of the implementation of the above two concepts, the free circulation of products originating in third countries inside the EC once they have been customs cleared in whatever port of entry of the EC custom territory.[2]

These rules would come to establish the Single European Market. Also, according to Article 119 of the Treaty on the Functioning of the European Union (TFEU) (ex Article 4 Treaty establishing the European Community—TEC),[3] trade policy should aim to achieve an open market economy with free competition. In addition, the aims of Article 206 (ex Article 131 TEC) are "to achieve the harmonious development of world trade, the progressive abolition of restrictions on international trade and the lowering of customs barriers." Despite these overtures, it was never clearly articulated to what extent the EU should liberalize trade. As I will discuss below, this ambiguity would have serious implications for decision-making when the scope of international trade rules extended to services, intellectual property rights, and investment.

From the outset, the EU was granted exclusive competency to elaborate, negotiate, and enforce all aspects of trade relations with third countries.[4] In bilateral, regional, and multilateral trade negotiations, the EU formally speaks with one voice and negotiates through one agent, the European Commission. Article 207 TFEU (ex Article 133 TEC) states that the EU retains exclusive competency over the CCP, which contains the provisions of EU external economic relations.

Historically, the GATT/WTO preferential trade agreements and domestic regulations pertaining to relations with third countries provided the basis for the CCP.[5] Although the EU was not a contracting party to the GATT in 1947, all of the member states were. Over the years the EU had acquired, for all intents and purposes, the status of a contracting party and the Commission negotiated on behalf of member states in successive rounds. Since 1970, the EU accepted most agreements negotiated within the GATT framework without acceptance by the individual member states as independent contractors.[6]

The EU's long-established system of exclusive competency was modeled after the practice of trade delegation to the collective level in advanced industrial democracies, such as the United States, where it had been shown "that such delegation helped insulate the policy-making process from domestic pressures, thus promoting a more liberal trade order."[7] The fiduciary logic of delegation also helps explain this system of competency. For Majone, the European Commission is both an agent and a fiduciary or trustee to whom a certain measure of independence is granted in the interest of achieving better quality policy outputs than would be possible if the European Commission only carried out member state directives.[8] According to this logic, the fiduciary is largely insulated from democratic notions of accountability that would inevitably constrain the efficiency of trade policymaking. Essentially, this system was designed to increase the EU's external influence in the creation and conclusion of trade agreements with third countries by presenting a common, unified front.

This system of exclusive competence only became contested once the creation of the WTO significantly broadened the scope of international trade. The expansion of multilateral trade rules into policies traditionally not "at the border" (e.g. tariffs and quotas) but inside the state (through national laws and regulations) forced an explicit internal EU debate on the issue of competence.

As noted above, Article 207 TFEU grants exclusive competence to the EU's legislative bodies (excluding the Parliament until the 2009 ToL) over the CCP. However, other than the requirement for uniformity and generalized statements regarding the progressive abolition of restrictions on international trade, Article 207 does not explicitly define the precise objectives or scope of commercial policy. The CCP was designed to cover trade in goods. The original architects of the EU did not anticipate that the scope of international trade rules would expand as it did. Therefore, the EU encountered an important constitutional problem. The issue was not so much whether the new WTO Agreements would be binding on EU member states (of course they would be), but which bodies would be responsible for interpreting and implementing the new rules into the EU and who would negotiate for Europe in subsequent negotiations on services, intellectual property rights, and investment.

In an effort to bring clarity to Article 207 TFEU (ex article 133 TEC), the European Court of Justice (ECJ) was asked by the European Commission for an "advisory opinion" on the issue of competence of the EU and the member states to negotiate, conclude, and implement WTO Agreements. The Commission lost this important case as Opinion 1/94[9] determined that the EU retains exclusive competency to negotiate and implement the Multilateral Agreement on Trade and Goods, but it shares mixed competence[10] with the member states on matters concerning the GATS and the Agreement on TRIPS.[11] This opinion is pursuant to the ECJ ruling that, "[o]nly in so far as common rules have been established at the internal level does the external competence of the Community become exclusive."[12] Therefore in order to avoid future competency disputes, the EU would have to amend the treaty either by enshrining mixed competency in the text or by explicitly expanding Article 207 TFEU (ex Article 133 TEC) to include "new issues."[13]

The Commission lobbied member states for extension of the EU's competency in all areas covered by the WTO Agreements on the basis that services account for over two-thirds of the European economy. The Commission insisted that all future trade deals would involve services and eventually member states would hold veto power over trade negotiations.[14] Moreover, mixed agreements were seen to be inefficient and to hinder the EU's bargaining strength in international trade negotiations.[15] The outcome was an amendment made by the Treaty of

Amsterdam that permitted the extension of the CCP to services and intellectual property rights without treaty reform, but only by a unanimous Council decision.

Under the leadership of EU Trade Commissioner Pascal Lamy, a compromise was struck at the 2001 Nice Summit between the minimalist option that would maintain the mixed competency status quo and the maximalist option that would communitarize trade in services and intellectual property rights negotiations. Exclusive competency became the general rule for trade in services. Competence would be shared only where "provisions for which unanimity is required for the adoption of internal rules or where it relates to a field in which the Community has not yet exercised the powers conferred upon it by this Treaty by adopting internal rules."[16] Also, a "cultural exception clause" required mixed competency in politically sensitive sectors—cultural, audiovisual services, education services, social services, and health services continue to be the subject of responsibility shared with the member states.[17] The commercial aspects of intellectual property fell under exclusive competence in the Nice Treaty and all other aspects of intellectual property would be shared.

The 2009 Treaty of Lisbon extends exclusive competency to the EU for all trade-related intellectual property but maintains exemptions for politically sensitive services. Article 207(4) TFEU provides for unanimity (mixed competency) in the fields of culture and audiovisual services where trade agreements "risk prejudicing the Union's linguistic and cultural diversity," and for social, education and health services, "where these agreements risk seriously disturbing the national organi[z]ation of such services and prejudicing the responsibility of Member States to deliver them." Whether member states will insist on unanimity in international trade negotiations in these areas remains untested. The most significant change brought about by the ToL is the extension of exclusive competence to the EU for foreign direct investment which had previously been mixed. Whether exclusive competence extends to liberalization or liberalization and investment protection remains unclear and contested, however.[18] The controversy over the inclusion of an investor-to-state dispute settlement mechanism in new mega-regional agreements such as the Comprehensive Economic Trade Agreement (CETA) and the Transatlantic Trade and Investment Partnership (TTIP) reflects this lack of clarity.[19]

The expanding competency of the EU is significant, not only because it shows how the EU exercises a consolidated voice in international trade negotiations but also because it explains why non-state actors increasingly set their sights on the EU institutions, particularly the Commission, to affect EU external trade policy.

Institutional dynamics in EU external trade governance[20]

The system of external trade policymaking in the EU is characterized by a two-tier delegation of authority that is consistent with the Community Method; decision-making involves all three EU-level institutions—Council, Commission, and Parliament—but the right of legislative initiative rests with the Commission.[21] In the first stage of delegation, the Commission drafts a proposed negotiating mandate for the EU that will set the parameters for international trade negotiations. DG Trade, in particular, works in consultation with other DGs—especially Development, Industry, and Agriculture—and non-state actors organized at the EU level to identify the objectives of the EU in international trade negotiations. The Commission also works closely with members of the Trade Policy Committee (TPC, formerly Article 133 Committee), which comprises senior trade officials from EU member states, to ensure the negotiating mandate reflects national, strategic interests and priorities. The function of the TPC is distinctive in that it coordinates member state positions on external trade, whereas the Committee of Permanent Representatives to the EU (COREPER) comprises generalist ambassadors and deputies who prepare Council meetings and are responsible for coordinating member states' positions on non-trade-related EU policy areas; COREPER defers to the TPC on matters of external trade. Once agreement is reached in the TPC, only the Council, acting on a proposal from the Commission, can formally approve the mandate and authorize the launch of negotiations in the Foreign Affairs Council (prior to the ToL, the General Affairs and External Relations Council). It can act by qualified majority voting in areas covered by exclusive EU competence, and unanimity in areas of mixed competency.[22] In practice, the Foreign Affairs Council operates by consensus. It is notable that the ToL did not extend any new, formal powers to the EP to authorize or set the objectives and parameters of international trade negotiations.

The Commission is then authorized to negotiate for the EU.[23] The role of the TPC at this stage is to act as the interface between the Commission negotiator and the EU member states. The TPC assists the Commission by making amendments to proposals for EU positions in ongoing external trade negotiations and generating member states' support for Commission lines. Given this important function, the TPC is characterized as the most active and powerful Council committee. Indeed, for some Commission officials, members of the TPC are their most important stakeholders who wield considerable influence over negotiations.[24] Members of civil society have critically characterized the TPC as a cog in a secret, technocratic decision-making scheme of EU external trade policymaking because it rarely makes its agendas public and the proceedings are kept behind closed doors.[25] These sentiments are reinforced by its opportunity to review unpublished Commission proposals and the tendency of national trade ministers to accept its recommendations, particularly those that pertain to more technical issues, without further debate in the Council.[26] Yet, beginning with Lamy, and continuing under successive DG Trade leaderships, fewer Commission resources have been committed to coordinating member state preferences.[27] Indeed, some TPC members claim they are beholden to the Commission's agenda and that it is nearly impossible to influence the substance of day-to-day negotiations. They feel that it is only when there is significant difference of opinion between a majority of member states, including the biggest ones, that they can really move the Commission.[28] Indeed, several candid senior Commission officials expressed views along the following lines:

> Member states are in the driving seat when setting parameters. Should the EU be willing to give up some agricultural subsidies? This is determined by member states. The Commission is in the driving seat for the day-to-day decision-making based on what is feasible for one country or a group of countries to swallow. I have been struck by how unimportant ... or how little attention Commission officials give member states, as long as their work falls within the parameters set by member states.[29]

These perceptions notwithstanding, the TPC functions by consensus and the Commission works to ensure member states broadly support its day-to-day agenda. Where it fails to do so, the TPC has the option of politicizing the issues in COREPER or at the Council level.

The ToL was aimed at improving the input legitimacy of the EU. One key measure was to enhance the role of the EP in the EU's external trade policymaking process by legally obliging the Commission to report on negotiations to the EP's specialist Committee on International Trade (INTA), which was created by the 2005–09 Parliament.[30] According to Article 218(10) TFEU, the EP "shall be immediately and fully informed at all stages of the negotiating procedure." Whereas the TPC is required to "assist" the Commission in negotiations, the TFEU grants the INTA consultative status.[31] Whether this implies a lower status for INTA is so far unclear.

Essentially, the ToL formalized the practice of involving the EP in day-to-day discussions regarding ongoing negotiations between the

Commission and the EP that began during Pascal Lamy's tenure as Trade Commissioner (1999–2004). Since then, DG Trade has tried to keep the EP abreast of all major developments in negotiations and to give members of the European Parliament (MEPs) written briefs and proposals for review, on par with the TPC. Lamy treated the EP as if it had more formal power than it did by consulting with democratically elected MEPs. This certainly went some distance towards improving the input legitimacy of EU external trade governance. However, the lack of trade expertise and institutional memory in INTA are two notable limits on the ability of the EP to engage or influence the course of negotiations compared with the TPC. Nonetheless, the ToL formalized the INTA as a key node in the external trade policymaking apparatus of the EU and therefore constitutes a focal point for some civil society activism on trade.

Once a trade agreement is reached, it must be adopted by the Council and, since the ToL, the EP. Prior to 2009, the EP's assent was only required if an agreement:

1   established specific institutional frameworks;
2   had budgetary implications;
3   required changes to EU legislation adopted by co-decision-making (i.e. when the Council and the EP were co-legislators); or
4   established an Association Agreement.[32]

The ToL extended co-decision—renamed the Ordinary Legislative Procedure (OLP) by the TFEU—to the implementation of the CCP and confirmed that the consent of the EP is required for all agreements, including trade, to which the OLP applies.[33] The EP must now grant its consent by a simple majority of MEPs before the Council formally adopts the results of negotiations by qualified majority voting for areas of the agreement covered by exclusive EU competence, and unanimity for areas of mixed or shared competence. As ever, national parliaments must also ratify those areas of agreement that are shared; however, their veto has shrunk considerably as the ToL extended exclusive EU competence to virtually all issues covered in international trade negotiations, with the few exceptions noted above.

The legal changes arising from the ToL to the status of the EP in the external trade policymaking process are significant, particularly with respect to codifying the involvement of democratically elected EU officials. However, given that the EP has no formal voice in setting the parameters of the negotiating mandate, the potential influence of MEPs is constrained by the agenda set by the Commission and the

Council; MEPs can only give assent to the agreement after all the negotiating partners sign on to it. Moreover, given its limited expertise and capacity to scrutinize Commission proposals, undertake research, conduct impact assessments, or make counter-proposals, the status quo will likely prevail, at least in the medium term; EP contributions will be in the form of political statements and interventions during negotiations and the Commission, and DG Trade in particular, will continue to shape and direct international trade negotiations. Unless, INTA develops greater trade-related expertise and non-state actors use the EP more regularly and strategically as a site for activism and lobbying in the future, the status quo will likely persist. Meanwhile, as competency has shifted to the EU level, the de facto autonomy of the Commission to lead EU trade diplomacy and serve as the sole voice of the EU in negotiations has grown exponentially, relative to the EP. This helps explain why the Commission, and particularly DG Trade, remains the target of trade-related activism at the EU level.

Political opportunities and non-state actors in EU trade politics

In 2009, the ToL enshrined the commitment to improve the input legitimacy of EU-level policymaking by requiring the EU institutions to consult with civil society organizations. Article 11 of the TFEU requires that:

1   The institutions shall, by appropriate means, give citizens and representative associations the opportunity to make known and publicly exchange their views in all areas of Union action.
2   The institutions shall maintain an open, transparent and regular dialogue with representative associations and civil society.
3   The European Commission shall carry out broad consultations with parties concerned in order to ensure that the Union's actions are coherent and transparent.

These commitments reflect a long-established practice in EU external trade governance. Indeed, beginning in 1999 and continuing to the present, EU policymakers have responded in significant ways to political contestation over trade liberalization and increasing demands for a voice by non-state actors in the external trade policymaking process. This section focuses on the formal mechanisms of consultation with non-state actors that have been concentrated in the Commission, particularly DG Trade. However, it is worth noting that non-state actors also have significant, informal relationships with the Council and the EP.

Member state positions in the Council reflect various stakeholders' aggregated interests and preferences that have been expressed at the national level.[34] At the EU level, members of the TPC engage in intense bargaining and often the decisions taken by Council bodies reflect the lowest common denominator between the most powerful EU member states.[35] However, while non-state actors may not sit in TPC meetings, there are informal relationships between member state representatives and industry associations such as the European Services Forum (ESF) and the European Roundtable of Industrialists (ERT). For example, the ESF organizes biannual meetings in which it invites members of the TPC and Commission officials to its head office[36] and the Commission has, in the past, orchestrated informal meetings between multinational water companies, and the TPC.[37] The extent of EU industry consultations with the TPC is unknown but it has caused NGOs over the years to demand more transparency in the TPC. For example, the World Wide Fund for Nature (WWF) has called for the inclusion of member state parliamentarians and MEPs in TPC meetings.[38] Many NGOs recommend that parliamentary reviews of the proceedings should occur at regular junctures. They also demand the publication of TPC agendas, records of decisions taken, and lists of all participants.[39]

In response, EU officials claim that these demands for transparency demonstrate a fundamental misunderstanding of trade negotiations. As one official explains:

> you cannot do trade policy fully transparently or we are only a postal service. Strategy must be private. We must have space to negotiate. There are so many leaks already coming out of [TPC] that the most contentious issues are not discussed there. If tomorrow, [TPC] was forced to become even more transparent, fewer and fewer issues would be discussed there.[40]

It is also noted that holding talks behind closed doors allows member state representatives to appear to represent their own constituencies, even when they are compelled to do otherwise (e.g. unable to get a qualified majority of states to force revision of Commission proposals).[41] For some EU officials, it is really up to non-state actors to initiate and generate informal relationships. NGOs, for example, could orchestrate meetings with Commission officials and members of TPC, just as industry does.[42] Some NGOs have made it a practice to approach trade counselors at the permanent representation in Brussels. Other well-established NGOs such as Oxfam contact incoming, rotating presidencies of the Council. These groups aim to assess the goals of incoming presidencies in order to prioritize their work appropriately. Nonetheless, these types of informal links are really more the exception than the rule among trade and development NGOs.

Though difficult to quantify, the relationships between the EP and non-state actors are more pronounced. EU-level NGOs have regular contact with MEPs, particularly those in INTA, who actively seek their input. For some, this can be linked to the democratic imperative—an effort by elected officials to convey the broader concerns of the public in trade policy discussions and recommendations. However, others attribute this relationship to the general lack of technical expertise amongst MEPs. For instance, one of the more vocal critics of the extension of co-decision powers to the EP once claimed, "[t]he day the constitution is ratified and the EP gets a vote is the demise of the EU trade policymaking process. It will become similar to the US Congress. There will be big competency problems, especially regarding services."[43] This reality has clearly not yet come to pass with the 2009 implementation of the ToL. Nonetheless, the EP is a voracious consumer of NGO papers. In the absence of sufficient trade-related expertise and capacity to read proposals and analysis critically, the EP is at risk of becoming little more than a postal service. And in comparison with the power wielded by the Commission, the voices of non-state actors working through the EP are tempests in teapots.

Formal consultative mechanisms for non-state actors

As noted above, the EU's formal consultative mechanisms for non-state actors are concentrated in the Commission. The Commission Secretariat-General develops the general approach of the Commission to civil society, works to establish guiding principles for consultation, and is responsible for the horizontal coordination of the Directorates-General.[44] Each DG then chooses its own consultative mechanisms according to its needs and engages non-state actors independently. The Commission has a long-standing commitment to consulting civil society and this has been increasingly formalized in recent years.

Responding to a series of legitimacy crises—widespread concern about public involvement, openness, and access to documents in the EU, criticism over the Commission's technocratic style of operations, the resignation of the Commission in 1999, the Irish "No" vote in its Nice Treaty ratification, and the low voter turnout and lack of public debate preceding the Nice Summit to name a few—the Commission conducted a number of assessments and consultations on non-state actors' involvement in EU governance beginning in 2001. The outcome White Paper became the basis for a set of general principles and minimum standards for consultations with non-state actors with which all DGs are required to comply.[45]

Box 2.1 General principles and minimum standards for European Commission consultations with interested parties

General principles

Participation

"The quality [...] of the EU policies implies wide participation by the citizens in each and every one of the different phases of the process, from policy conception to policy implementation."

Openness and accountability

"The [European] institutions should work in a more open manner [...] in order to improve the confidence in complex institutions."
"Each of the EU institutions must explain and take responsibility for what it does in Europe."

Effectiveness

"Policies must be effective and timely, delivering what is needed."

Coherence

"Policies and actions must be coherent."

Minimum standards

Clear content of the consultation process

"All communications relating to consultations should be clear and concise, and should include all necessary information to facilitate response."

Consultation target groups

"When defining the target group(s) in a consultation process, the Commission should ensure that relevant parties have an opportunity to express their opinions."

Publication

"The Commission should ensure adequate awareness-raising publicity and adapt its communication channels to meet the needs of target audiences. Without excluding other communication tools, open public consultations should be published on the internet and announced in a 'single access point'."

Time limits for participation

"The Commission should provide sufficient time for planning and responses to invitations and written contributions. The Commission should strive to allow at least 8 weeks for reception of responses to written public consultations and 20 working days notice for meetings."

European Commission, "General Principles and Minimum Standards for Consultation of Interested Parties by the Commission," COM (2002): 704.

Since the DGs are autonomous units, there is no Commission-wide or uniform approach to implementing these principles and standards. This has led to "a patchy picture of civil society dialogue"[46] emerging across the DGs. However, the Commission has developed a number of mechanisms designed to help the DGs meet these broadly defined "soft" policy objectives. For example, the Commission's "Better Lawmaking" activities help the DGs develop more coherent policy proposals for consideration by non-state actors.[47] In this vein, the Commission conducts assessments of the likely social, environmental, and economic impact of proposed policy actions and regulations.[48] The purpose is to generate a "culture of feedback and review to learn from the successes and mistakes of the past ... [and to] ensure proposals do not over-regulate and that the decisions are taken and implemented at the appropriate level."[49] In part, impact assessments are intended to structure and generate broad debates with a range of interested parties over proposed policies and regulations.[50]

The Commission created "Your Voice in Europe"[51] as part of the Interactive Policymaking Initiative (IPM) in 2001, thereby following through with its commitment to develop a single access point through which it could communicate with non-state actors. This Internet portal enables the Commission to solicit participation and publish the results of public consultations, gives EU citizens, consumers, and businesses the opportunity to express their opinions about proposed EU policies, facilitates chat sessions between EU citizens and EU officials, and permits personal testimony regarding "on the ground" impacts of EU policies. Internet consultation was really a revolutionary and unprecedented effort to bridge the gap between ordinary citizens and policymakers which has dramatically increased public involvement in EU policymaking since its inception in 2001.

The Commission also introduced a "Transparency Initiative" to make more readily available information about lobbying in Brussels and thereby improve the transparency, integrity, and credibility of EU policymaking. As part of this initiative, in 2011, the EP and the Commission launched a joint public transparency register aimed at disclosing information about EU lobbyists and the interests they pursue.[52]

Most recently, Article 11(4) Treaty on European Union (TEU) provided for the creation of a European Citizens' Initiative (ECI):

> Not less than one million citizens who are nationals of a significant number of Member States may take the initiative of inviting the European Commission, within the framework of its powers, to submit any appropriate proposal on matters where citizens consider that a legal act of the Union is required for the purpose of implementing the Treaties.

In practice, the ECI functions much like a right to petition the European Commission. Since 2012, over 20 different initiatives have been launched, three of which have successfully garnered over 1 million signatures of support from a significant number of member states—Right to Water, One of Us, and Stop Vivisection—and are being considered by the Commission. The hope is that the process of generating signatures and statements of support will lead to wide-ranging, collective debate across the EU on common areas of concern, thereby contributing to deliberative democracy. It is too soon to tell whether these lofty goals will be achieved by the initiative, but it does represent a dramatic attempt to involve citizens in the EU's legislative agenda.[53]

Non-state actors and the Civil Society Dialogue

The Commission-wide guidelines, principles, and mechanisms discussed above provide the backdrop for DG Trade relations with non-state actors. Most significant is the Civil Society Dialogue (CSD), which provides for regular, structured consultations between senior DG Trade officials and a range of economic and non-economic, non-state actors.[54] In the aftermath of the failed Seattle Ministerial in 1999, DG Trade launched the CSD. From the start, improving the input legitimacy of EU external trade policymaking was the explicit goal:

1 *To consult widely*: the Commission wants to take into account the views of all interested parties when drafting proposals and action.
2 *To address civil society concerns on trade policy*: as globalization obviously raised concerns for many in society, the Commission wanted to find out more about these concerns, debate specific issues, answer questions where possible and take up suggestions for actions made by CSDs.
3 *To improve EU trade policymaking through structured dialogue*: debating the questions that are shaping public opinion as a way of updating and strengthening the Commission's expertise, which is important as these issues also have an impact on public acceptance of trade policy.
4 *To improve transparency*: by engaging in a dialogue with civil society and making documents available on its website, DG Trade is looking to achieve greater transparency (of the trade policymaking process).[55]

Further, a 2014 independent evaluation provided an overview of the desired intervention logic of the CSD (see Figure 2.1).

The CSD involves regular meetings between DG Trade officials and registered members of civil society on EU trade policy. A contact group was created in 2000 to serve as a steering committee that would identify key issues for consultation and act as a sounding board for Commission proposals. It acts as a mediator between the Commission and other registered members of the CSD, and monitors CSD compliance with its stated objectives. As a general practice, members of the contact group have also participated alongside Commission officials at WTO ministerial conferences. Membership in the contact group has remained relatively constant.[56] The most significant change has been the decline in participation by NGOs and consumer organizations since 2007. Today it includes five business associations, one agriculture association, one trade union association, two NGOs, and the European Economic and Social Committee (EESC).[57]

The CSD is open to registered participants and, since 2004, most meetings have been ad hoc, corresponding to important developments in international trade negotiations. Topics relating to the Doha Development Agenda (DDA) dominated the CSD agenda until multilateral negotiations stalled in 2008. The focus of discussions has since shifted

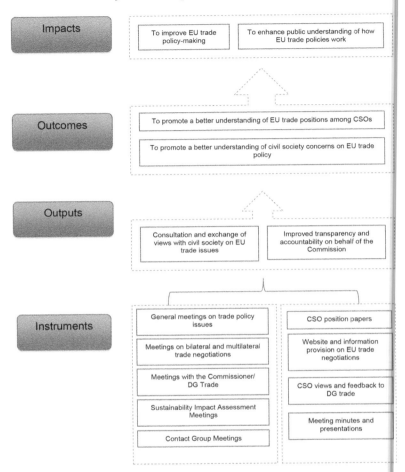

Figure 2.1 DG Trade's Civil Society Dialogue—desired intervention logic

to bilateral and mega-regional negotiations. The frequency of meetings has also declined over time; during the first 10 years of the CSD an average of 33 meetings took place but that has since dropped to 19.[58]

Participation in the CSD meetings has also waned. In the early days, participants reported very high levels of interest and engagement.[59] Over time, consultation fatigue and disillusion with the CSD and the lack of progress in the DDA have characterized the process. As a consequence the number of organizations registered for and participating in CSD meetings has sharply declined. In 2008 more than 800 participants were registered but it was estimated by independent eva-luators that only 350, or 43 percent of organizations routinely partici-pated in CSD meetings.[60] The CSD annual reports conducted by DG Trade show fluctuations in registrations: 836 in 2010;[61] 863 in 2011;[62] 515 in 2012;[63] and 655 in 2013.[64] A second independent evaluation of the CSD reported that only 359 were registered in 2014.[65] The number increased slightly by May 2015 to 423.[66] A close look at the participants lists at CSD meetings shows that approximately 30 participants have attended each meeting since 2001 but the number of NGOs is declining relative to business associations. The Transparency Register also shows that there are far more in-house lobbyists, trade and business associations registered for the CSD in 2015 than NGOs (see Figure 2.2).

This situation is owing in part to the centrality of bilateral and mega-regional trade negotiations to the EU's external trade agenda, and also to the growing levels of dissatisfaction with the CSD and the lack of progress in multilateral trade negotiations among NGOs. Two independent evaluations of the CSD conducted in 2007 and 2014 concur that the process is best characterized as an "information relay" or briefing exercise than a forum to debate trade-related priorities or influence the content of policy.[67] While DG Trade officials are able to hear the views of participants, NGO participants have long expressed frustration over the lack of debate in the CSD and their inability to influence the trade agenda:

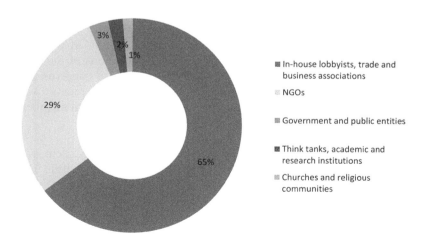

Figure 2.2a Active organizations registered with the Civil Society Dialogue

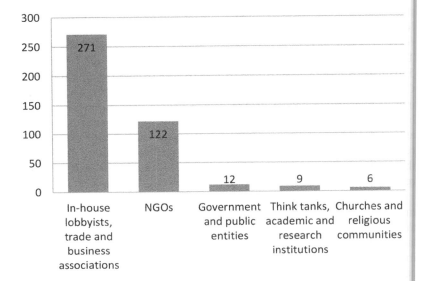

Figure 2.2b Active organizations registered with the Civil Society Dialogue
*Note on methodology: The 420 registrants were active in the CSD as of 8
May 2015. The classifications were based directly from the organization's pro-
file in the Transparency Registrar, available at http://ec.europa.eu/transpa
rencyregister/public/homePage.do.

> DG Trade is one of the most advanced in generating consultation
> with civil society. On the other hand the level of dialogue is quite
> weak. The CSD is essentially an information session. Most meet-
> ings include the presentation of briefs and discussions of the state
> of play. [Participants] have the opportunity to raise concerns and
> questions but they rarely receive concrete replies. There is no will
> from the Commission to listen to concrete proposals from members
> of civil society—particularly NGOs—in this context.[68]

These sentiments are repeated in the 2007 and 2014 independent evaluations and, to date, there seems to be little willingness within DG
Trade to change the format or objectives. In response, some NGOs
have explicitly opted out of participating in the CSD.[69]

These shortcomings notwithstanding, the CSD is an ambitious effort
to increase the involvement of non-state actors in the EU's external trade
policymaking process. There is a clear commitment within DG Trade
to engage with a range of non-state actors from all sectors and to

subject trade policy proposals to structured, public scrutiny, at least in the latter stages of their development. DG Trade officials regularly inform CSD participants about the development of policies, provide ongoing updates of developments and state of play in trade negotiations, and respond to questions. In this way, the CSD encourages mutual understanding of concern and demystifies international trade negotiations. In some instances, DG Trade officials rely on non-state actors to filter information, expertise, and public opinion upwards to the EU level, thereby serving as the eyes and ears of the Commission. In addition to improving the mutual knowledge deficit, the CSD adds transparency and accountability to the partnership by subjecting the dialogue to continuous review. Therefore, the CSD fits well with the Commission's overall commitment to transparency and good governance.

DG Trade consultations with economic, non-state actors

DG Trade has well established, formal relations with economic, non-state actors that take place alongside the CSD. Perhaps most significant is its relationship with the European social partners—the Union of Industrial and Employers' Confederations of Europe (UNICE), European Centre of Enterprises with Public Participation and of Enterprises of General Economic Interest (CEEP), and the European Trade Union Confederation (ETUC)—which lobby on matters concerning employment, social affairs, and macroeconomic policy and whose relationship with the Commission is defined in the TFEU under the terms of the European Social Dialogue.[70] DG Trade regularly consults the ETUC and UNICE throughout all stages of external trade policymaking. DG Trade officials meet regularly with members of UNICE's international relations committee and UNICE is part of the official EU delegation at WTO ministerial meetings, as are all members of the CSD contact group. The ETUC enjoys many of the same opportunities for consultation, especially in areas of particular concern to its members, such as the movement of service suppliers across borders. These opportunities notwithstanding, the social partners have expressed concern that their influence over trade is being diluted by the increased involvement of other economic, non-state actors in the EU's external trade policymaking process.[71]

Since 1995, DG Trade has stepped up its efforts to foster and enhance its relationship with the private sector. In part, this has involved developing intimate, consultative, and partnership arrangements with several business forums, especially the ESF and the Trans-Atlantic

Business Dialogue (TABD)/Trans-Atlantic Business Council (TABC). The ESF works to advance the interests of the European services industries in multilateral, regional, and bilateral trade negotiations. As of May 2015, the membership list includes 32 European and national services federations and 22 multinational companies.[72] Its core objectives are to encourage liberalized service markets throughout the world, to remove trade and investment barriers, and to improve market access for service industries through trade negotiations.[73] Created in 1999 at the behest of the European Commission, the ESF advises DG Trade on trade in services negotiations. At the launch of the ESF, Trade Commissioner Leon Brittan characterized the relationship between DG Trade and the ESF thus:

> You are the driving force of the consultation system which we have established, my door is open for any matters of concern [...] I am in your hand[s] to listen to what are your objectives, your priorities for liberalization [...] I count on your support and input, at the company, CEO and Chairman as well as the European or National Federations levels, so that we can refine our strategy and set out clear, priority negotiating objectives which will make a difference in the international expansion of services business.[74]

To fulfill this role, the ESF prepares position papers and serves as a member of the CSD contact group. ESF Managing Director Pascal Kerneis participates regularly in CSD meetings and accompanies DG Trade officials to WTO ministerial meetings. DG Trade officials also regularly brief the ESF on ongoing services negotiations and seek feedback on confidential documents, such as requests for third country market access.[75] Individual members of the ESF also have regular, informal contact with DG Trade officials where the opportunity to influence EU services offers and requests has been described as "significant."[76]

In another effort to strengthen public-private partnerships, the TABD was created by EU and US government officials in 1995 as part of the New Transatlantic Agenda (NTA)[77] and later reaffirmed in 1998 in the New Economic Partnership.[78] The TABD is designed to facilitate dialogue between the CEOs of European and American multinational corporations, and EU and US policymakers on how best to liberalize trade. In 2013, the TABD became the executive council of the TABC.[79] The TABC is described as "the only CEO-driven business organization solely dedicated to advancing the US-EU economic agenda [by providing] its member executives high-level access to US

Cabinet Secretaries and European Commissioners."[80] In the EU, DG Enterprise and Industry coordinates relations with the TABC in cooperation with DG Trade and DG External Relations. Consultations with US and EU businesses take place during an annual conference in which over 100 CEOs and senior-level government representatives participate. A second, large-scale meeting traditionally takes place at the World Economic Forum in Davos. Frequent policy committee meetings are also held throughout the year. For Cowles, the TABD/TABC "blurs the traditional distinction between public and private governance, with businessmen effectively negotiating in quadrilateral forums alongside their governmental counterparts."[81]

The creation of forums like the ESF and the TABD/TABC marks an institutional innovation that created entirely new and private access points through which industry representatives can interact with EU policymakers without interference from other non-state actors. Unlike more traditional, self-organized industrial lobbies such as the ERT, the TABD/TABC and the ESF were created at the behest of Commission officials. They are forums where the status of industry is elevated from the standard "ad hoc advisory groups convened to elicit private-sector opinion on specific instances of policymaking," to institutionalized interlocutors endowed with the right to "generate [their] own coordinated agenda for policy change" and who enjoy a relatively autonomous right of initiative to set and influence the external trade agenda.[82]

Conclusion

This chapter has outlined the context within which non-state actors—including economic actors such as business associations and non-economic actors such as NGOs—seek to influence the EU's external trade agenda. Expanding, exclusive competency for the EU combined with changing institutional dynamics and growing democratic powers for the EP help explain why the EU—as opposed to national governments—is increasingly the target of trade-related activism by non-state actors. Moreover, the EU is driven by a robust cosmopolitan, democratic imperative to give voice to those affected by its policies. The dramatic and unprecedented efforts to make external trade policymaking more participatory, accountable, and transparent make the EU a ripe environment for assessing the impact of NGO advocacy and campaigning. The next two chapters provide detailed analyses of the role of NGOs in the EU's external trade policymaking process in two very different cases—one in which they leveraged these opportunities to advocate from within the political process and one in which NGOs explicitly rejected these new political opportunities and protested from the streets and in the media. Surprisingly, the cases in Chapters 3 and 4 show that both groups of NGOs were able to improve the quality of decision-making but the institutional dynamics, political opportunities, and imbalances in access between economic and non-economic actors discussed here make little difference in terms of whether NGOs successfully influence external trade policy.

Notes

1 At the WTO, the European Commission negotiates on behalf of the European Union and the 28 individual member states.
2 Stefano Inama and Edwin Vermulst, *Customs and Trade Laws of the European Community* (London: Kluwer Law International, 1999), 5.
3 In this book, I use the 2012 consolidated versions of the Treaty on European Union (TEU) and the Treaty on the Functioning of the European Union (TFEU), unless otherwise specified.
4 As opposed to a system of mixed competence where authority is granted on "an ad hoc basis and for negotiating purposes ... [and] individual member states retain a veto both through unanimity voting in the Council and through ratification by their own national parliaments." See Sophie Meunier and Kalypso Nicolaïdis, "Who Speaks for Europe? The Delegation of Trade Authority in the EU," *Journal of Common Market Studies* 37, no. 3 (1999): 482.
5 Thomas Cottier, "Towards a Common External Economic Policy of the European Union," in *European Yearbook of International Economic Law: Common Commercial Policy after Lisbon*, ed. Marc Bungenberg and Christoph Hermann (New York: Springer, 2013), 3–15.
6 Exceptions include two agreements at the end of the Tokyo Round and the part of the Tariff Protocol relating to the European Coal and Steel Community products. See Jacques H.J. Bourgeois, "The Tokyo Round Agreements on Technical Barriers and on Government Procurement," *Common Market Law Review* 19, no. 1 (1982): 22, for further discussion.
7 Meunier and Nicolaïdis, "Who Speaks for Europe?," 480.
8 See especially, Giandomenico Majone, "Two Logics of Delegation: Agency and Fiduciary Relations in EU Governance," *European Union Politics* 2, no. 1 (2001): 103–122.
9 European Communities, "Competence of the Community to Conclude International Agreements Concerning Services and the Protection of Intellectual Property—Article 228 (6) of the EC Treaty," *Opinion 1/94, European Court Ruling I-5267*, 1994.
10 Mixed agreements, those combining EU and member state competence, require ratification by member state parliaments.
11 For a legal analysis of the Court's advisory opinion, see Jacques H.J. Bourgeois, "The EC in the WTO and Advisory Opinion 1/94: An Echternach Procession," *Common Market Law Review* 32, no. 3 (1995): 763–787; and Meinhard Hilf, "The ECJ's Opinion 1/94 on the WTO: No Surprise, but Wise?," *European Journal of International Law* 6, no. 2 (1995): 245–259.

12 European Community, "Competence of the Community to Conclude International Agreements Concerning Services and the Protection of Intellectual Property," at paragraph 77. However, in paragraph 85, the Court accepts that very exceptional external powers may become exclusive without a prior exercise of internal powers.

13 European Community, "Competence of the Community to Conclude International Agreements Concerning Services and the Protection of Intellectual Property."

14 See Marise Cremona, "External Commercial Policy After Amsterdam: Authority and Interpretation within Interconnected Legal Orders," in *The EU, The WTO and NAFTA: Towards a Common Law of International Trade*, ed. Joseph H.H. Weiler (Oxford: Oxford University Press, 2000), for a more thorough analysis of the legislative history and the scope of Article 133 and the implications of its amendment for the future of European external economic policy.

15 European Commission, "Adjustment of Article 113," DG I, Intergovernmental Conference Personnel Representatives (I/330/96), 16 October 1996. Cited in Meunier and Nicolaïdis, "Who Speaks for Europe?," 494.

16 EU-Lex, "Treaty establishing the European Community (Consolidated Version, 2002) [TEC]," *Official Journal of the European Union*, C 325, 24 December 2002, Article 133(5). Notably the language of this article changed in the TFEU to reflect the expanding competency of the EU.

17 Article 133(6) TEC.

18 Julien Chaisse, "Promises and Pitfalls of the European Union Policy on Foreign Investment—How Will the New EU Competence on FDI affect the Emerging Global Regime?," *Journal of International Economic Law* 15, no. 1: 51–84; and Sophie Meunier, "Divide and Conquer? China and the Cacophony of Foreign Investment Rules in the EU," *Journal of European Public Policy* 21, no. 7 (2014): 996–1016.

19 Ferdi de Ville and Gabriel Siles-Brügge, *TTIP: The Truth about the Transatlantic Trade and Investment Partnership* (Cambridge: Polity Press, forthcoming).

20 The history of the EU's external trade policymaking process is well documented by Stephen Woolcock, *European Union Economic Diplomacy: The Role of the EU in External Economic Relations* (Farnham: Ashgate Publishing, 2013); Sophie Meunier and Kalypso Nicolaïdis, "The European Union as a Conflicted Trade Power," *Journal of European Public Policy* 13, no. 6 (2006): 906–925; and Alasdair R. Young and John Peterson, "The EU and the New Trade Politics," *Journal of European Public Policy* 13, no. 6 (2006): 795–814.

21 EUR-Lex, "Consolidated Version of the Treaty on the Functioning of the European Union (TFEU)," *Official Journal of the European Union*, C 326, 26 November 2012, Article 207.

22 EUR-Lex, "Consolidated Version of the Treaty on the Functioning of the European Union (TFEU)."

23 EUR-Lex, "Consolidated Version of the Treaty on the Functioning of the European Union (TFEU)."

24 Interview with Senior Trade Policy Official, Unit DG Trade, G1—Trade in Services and Investment, General Agreement on Trade in Services (GATS) and Investment, 8 October 2004.

25 See WWF, "A League of Gentlemen: Who Really Runs EU Trade Decision Making?," WWF-UK Research Center, 2003.

26 Non-controversial issues, called A-points, are not discussed further by the Council once approved by COREPER.

27 According to one DG Trade official, in the past "the Commission would spend around 80 percent of its resources trying to coordinate member state preferences and 20 percent of its time and resources would be spent on external affairs. Under Lamy, the opposite has been true." Interview with Desk Officer, DG Trade, G1—Trade in Services and Investment, GATS and Investment, 8 October 2004.

28 Interview with Permanent Member State Representative, Former Chair of Committee 133, 4 October 2004.

29 Interview with Desk Officer—Policy and negotiations, DG Trade, Unit F1— Coordination of WTO, OECD [Organisation for Economic Co-operation and Development], Trade-Related Assistance; GATT; and 133 Committee, 12 October 2004.

30 Prior to 2005, DG Trade reported to a more generalist EP committee that also represented industry and energy.

31 Article 207(3) TFEU.

32 Stephen Woolcock, *European Union Economic Diplomacy, 60.*

33 Article 207 TFEU and Article 218 TFEU (ex Article 300 TEC), respectively.

34 Andrew Moravcsik, "Taking Preferences Seriously: A Liberal Theory of International Politics," *International Organization* 51, no. 4 (1997): 513–553; and Helen Milner, *Resisting Protectionism: Global Industries and the Politics of International Trade* (Princeton, N.J.: Princeton University Press, 1988).

35 Andrew Moravcsik, *The Choice for Europe: Social Purpose and State Power from Messina to Maastricht* (Ithaca, NY: Cornell University Press, 1998); and Robert Putnam, "Diplomacy and Domestic Politics: The Logic of Two-Level Games," *International Organization* 42, no. 3 (1988): 427–460.

36 Email between Joao Machado Aguiar, Head of Unit DG Trade, G1— Trade in Services and Investment; GATS and Investment to Pascal Kerneis, Director of the European Services Forum, 31 October 2003. This correspondence was confirmed as accurate by an interview with Senior Trade Policy Official working in DG Trade, G1—Trade in Services and Investment; GATS and Investment, 14 June 2005.

37 Christina Deckwirth, "Water Almost Out of GATS?," *A Corporate Europe Observatory Briefing*, 2006, 4.

38 WWF, "A League of Gentlemen"

39 "Transparency in European Trade Policy-Making," Joint Statement by European Civil Society, *Germanwatch*, 2003, germanwatch.org/tw/transp03.htm.

40 Senior Official, DG Trade Unit A2—Inter-institutional Relations and Communications Policy, interview by author, 29 September 2004.

41 Interview with Senior Trade Policy Official, Unit DG Trade, G1—Trade in Services and Investment; GATS and Investment, 8 October 2004.

42 Interview with Senior Trade Policy Official, DG Trade, G1—Trade in Services and Investment; GATS and Investment, 14 June 2005.

43 Interview with Pascal Kerneis, Director of the European Services Forum, 24 September 2004. Concerns about MEPs' trade policy competence are echoed in several interviews with EU officials and Permanent Member State Representatives but the general view among them is that more power for the EP will translate into more incentive for MEPs to educate themselves about trade, in the long term.

44 The Commission's general approach to engaging civil society is well documented in Beate Kholer-Koch and Christine Quittkat, *De-Mystification of Participatory Democracy: EU Governance and Civil Society* (Oxford: Oxford University Press, 2013); Meike Rodekamp, *Their Members' Voices: Civil Society Organizations in the European Union* (Weisbaden, Germany: Springer VS, 2013), and Luis Bouza Garcia, *Participatory Democracy and Civil Society in the EU: Agenda Setting and Institutionalization* (Basingstoke: Palgrave Macmillan, 2015).

45 The paper suggests (among other things) the need for stronger interactions with civil society, with recommendations for greater openness and inclusion (e.g. establishing minimum standards for consultation). European Commission, "European Governance: A White Paper," COM(2001) 428 Final, 2.

46 Elodie Fazi and Jeremy Smith, "Civil Society Dialogue: Making it Work Better," *Study Commissioned by the Civil Society Contact Group*, 2006.

47 European Commission, "European Governance: Better Lawmaking," COM(2002) 275 Final.

48 See European Commission, "Impact Assessment Guidelines," SEC(2005) 791.

49 European Commission, Governance Team, "Report of Working Group: Consultation and Participation of Civil Society," *White Paper on European Governance, Work Area no. 2: Handling the Process of Producing and Implementing Community Rules*, 2001.

50 European Communities, "Regulation (EC) No. 1049/2001 of the European Parliament and of the Council of 30 May 2001 Regarding Public Access to European Parliament, Council and Commission Documents," *Official Journal of the European Communities*, L145/43, 2001.

51 Your Voice in Europe, last updated 30 June 2014, ec.europa.eu/yourvoice/.

52 Transparency Register, last updated 29 April 2015, ec.europa.eu/transparencyregister/public/homePage.do?redir=false&locale=en.

53 Maria Lee, *EU Environmental Law, Governance, and Decision-Making*, second edition (Oxford: Hart Publishing, 2014), 187–189.

54 A detailed overview of the history and evolution of the CSD is provided by Annette Slob and Floor Smakman, "A Voice not a Vote: Evaluation of the Civil Society Dialogue at DG Trade," an independent review commissioned by the European Commission, Directorate-General for Trade (ECORYS Nederland BV, 2007), trade.ec.europa.eu/doclib/docs/2007/march/tradoc_133527.pdf.

55 DG Trade, "Factsheet: Civil Society Dialogue—How and Why," quoted in Slob and Smakman, "A Voice Not a Vote," 24.

56 The Network for Women in Development (WIDE) replaced the European Public Health Alliance (EPHA) in 2005 but no longer participates. Two other NGOs, the WWF and SOLIDAR, withdrew after 2007. The UNICE and the Bureau Européen des Unions de Consommateurs (BEUC) are also no longer included.

57 Members in 2015 include: ACT Alliance Advocacy to the European Union (formerly APRODEV), BUSINESSEUROPE, Eurochambres, European Services Forum, European Trade Union Confederation, EuroCommerce, Eurogroup for Animals, European Economic and Social Committee (EESC), Comité des Organisations Professionnelles Agricoles de l'Union Européenne (COPA), and European Foreign Trade Association.

58 A complete list of meetings and participants is available at trade.ec.europa. eu/civilsoc/meetlist.cfm.

59 Eva Kaluzynska, Former Policy Desk Officer responsible for Civil Society Dialogue, DG Trade, Unit G3: Sustainable Development/Civil Society Dialogue, email correspondence with author, 2 October 2006.

60 Slob and Smakman, "A Voice Not a Vote," 11.

61 Directorate-General for Trade, "DG Trade Civil Society Dialogue—Report of Activities in 2010," European Commission, 2011, trade.ec.europa.eu/ doclib/docs/2010/february/tradoc_145785.pdf.

62 Directorate-General for Trade, "Annual Report of Activities 2011—Civil Society Dialogue on Trade," European Commission, 2012, trade.ec.europa. eu/doclib/docs/2012/january/tradoc_148960.pdf.

63 Directorate-General for Trade, "Annual Report 2012—Civil Society Dialogue on Trade; Summary of Activities in 2012," European Commission, bookshop.europa.eu/en/home/.

64 Directorate-General for Trade, "Annual Report 2013—Civil Society Dialogue on Trade," European Commission, 2014.

65 Melanie Kitchener, "Evaluation of DG Trade's Civil Society Dialogue in Order to Assess its Effectiveness, Efficiency and Relevance," an independent review commissioned by the European Commission, Directorate-General for Trade, *Coffey International Development*, 28 July 2014, trade. ec.europa.eu/doclib/docs/2014/december/tradoc_152927.pdf.

66 See organizations registered with the CSD at trade.ec.europa.eu/civilsoc/sea rch.cfm?action=form.

67 Slob and Smakman, "A Voice Not a Vote"; and Melanie Kitchener, "Evaluation of DG Trade's Civil Society Dialogue."

68 Interview with Guillame Legaut, Trade and Food Security Advocacy Officer, Development, Coopération Internationale pour le Développement et la Solidarité (CIDSE), 2 June 2005.

69 See for example the following 2009 letter by the Seattle to Brussels Network to Catherine Ashton, EU Commissioner for External Trade, www.wa ronwant.org/attachments/letter_from_s2b_to_ashton_on_csd_may09.pdf.

70 Articles 154 and 155 TFEU (ex Articles 138–139 TEC).

71 Interview with WTO Advisor, Union of Industrial and Employers' Confederations of Europe (UNICE), 24 September 2004.

72 European Services Forum, "Members," www.esf.be/new/who-we-are/members/.

73 See European Services Forum, www.esf.be.

74 Sir Leon Brittan, "European Services Leaders' Group," Speech launching European Services Network, European Commission: Office of Sir Leon Brittan, 26 January 1999.

75 For example, in one email DG Trade—Services, Head of Unit João Aguiar Machado wrote to Pascal Kerneis, Managing Director of the ESF: "[W]e would very much welcome industry's input to this exercise, both in terms of finding out where the problems currently lie and in making specific

requests. Without ESF input the exercise risks becoming a purely intellectual one ..." He then sent Pascal Kerneis a reminder, stressing "the importance to provide within the following days any input you [i.e. the ESF] may have, as we are currently finali[z]ing the draft requests that will be transmitted to Member States very soon." These emails were ascertained by the NGO, Corporate Europe Observatory through EU access to documents requests.

76 Interview with Peter McNamee, Legal Advisor, Council of Bars and Law Societies of Europe (CCBE), 10 June 2005; interview with Marc Pouw, Secretary-General, Association of European Public Postal Operators (PostEurop), 16 June 2005; and interview with Mark van der Horst, Chairman, Competition and Market Reform Committee, European Express Association (EEA), 7 June 2005.

77 For the text of this agenda see European Union, "New Transatlantic Agenda," Delegation of the European Commission to the United States, 1995; and European Union, "Joint EU/US Action Plan," Delegation of the European Commission to the United States, 1995.

78 European Commission, "Transatlantic Economic Partnership: Action Plan," DG Trade: External Relations, 1998.

79 See Trans-Atlantic Business Council, www.transatlanticbusiness.org.

80 See Trans-Atlantic Business Council, "About TABD," www.transatlantic business.org/tabd/about-tabd/.

81 Maria Green Cowles, "The Transatlantic Business Dialogue: Transforming the New Transatlantic Dialogue," in *Transatlantic Governance in a Global Economy*, ed. Mark Pollack and Gregory Shaffer (Lanham, MD: Rowman and Littlefield, 2001), 214.

82 Richard Sherman and Johan Eliasson, "Trade Disputes and Non-State Actors: New Institutional Arrangements and the Privatization of Commercial Diplomacy," *The World Economy* 29, no. 4 (2006): 475.

3 Prescription for influence?

NGOs and the EU's TRIPS, and access to medicines negotiations[1]

- Locking intellectual property rights into the multilateral trade regime
- NGOs bring the Access to Medicines Campaign to the EU
- Negotiating a solution to the Paragraph 6 Problem
- Conclusion

Following the conclusion of the Uruguay Round of multilateral trade negotiations in 1994, and the subsequent entry into force of the Agreement on Trade-Related Intellectual Property Rights in 1995, NGOs waged a sustained campaign aimed at ensuring the primacy of public health over intellectual property rights (IPR). The global Access to Medicines movement is heralded by scholars and activists alike as evidence of NGOs' ability to influence international public policy.[2] Rather than focus on the international dimension of this campaign, as much of the existing literature on the subject has done, this chapter traces the role of NGOs in the formulation of the EU's position on trade-related IPR and access to medicines.[3] I argue that although NGOs have been instrumental in providing education, raising awareness, and giving a voice to broader societal concerns about the social and health-related aspects of proposed trade deals, EU policymakers did not pursue policies that placed public health concerns over IPR protection, despite NGO involvement in the external trade policymaking process. This failure is owing to the robust normative framework within which negotiations took place.

The TRIPS Agreement ushered in fundamental normative and substantive changes in the global IPR regime. By codifying, legalizing, and linking intellectual property rules to the international trade regime, WTO members severely constrained the range of policy options that would be considered appropriate in subsequent TRIPS negotiations and thereby determined the future pattern of consultation and dialogue between NGOs and EU policymakers.[4] Early optimism regarding the power of NGOs to bring about substantive, normative changes in the international IPR regime was premature. The evidence, particularly following the Doha Declaration in 2001, suggests that EU policymakers acquiesced to certain NGO demands by making incremental—at least as far as developing and least-developed countries were concerned—changes in the least vital areas or by clarifying already existing rules in the international IPR regime to maintain a forward momentum in WTO trade negotiations. Once the pressure from NGOs lessened and the issues became more technical, EU policymakers shifted back to their preferred set of hard-line, market-oriented outcomes on IPR. Experts and technocrats, not NGOs or firms and business associations, were empowered in the EU's external trade policymaking process to maintain and reinforce the status quo. As the issue became more complex and technical by virtue of the so-called "Paragraph 6 Problem," experts and technocrats gained greater functional authority to find a solution that fit inside and, indeed, reproduced the legal-liberal episteme of the international trade regime.

This chapter assesses the role of NGOs in the development of the EU's position on access to medicines in two parts. The first section examines the development of the EU's position leading up to the 2001 Doha Declaration and the role played by NGOs in educating both the public and EU-level policymakers about the links between stringent IPR protection and the AIDS crisis in Africa. NGOs were empowered at this stage of decision-making, which was characterized by highly politicized debates about the appropriate circumstances under which to invoke mechanisms such as compulsory licenses and parallel importation to battle public health crises. Second, efforts to solve the Paragraph 6 Problem, a hang over from the Doha Declaration, are examined. During this stage, policy discussions centered on the highly technical matter of deciding how to ensure countries with no domestic manufacturing capacity could secure adequate access to affordable medicines. As the issues became more complex and NGOs became more critical of the hard-line market-oriented proposals on the table, DG Trade experts and technocrats pulled away from the participatory process and effectively sidelined NGOs at this stage of policy development. This chapter shows that while NGOs certainly improved the procedural legitimacy of external trade policymaking, they were unable to influence the substance of policy such that it prioritizes public health and welfare over commercial priorities and IPR protection.

Locking intellectual property rights into the multilateral trade regime

The TRIPS Agreement effectively shifted the IPR regime into the legal-liberal episteme and locked in minimum standards for IPR protection for WTO members. Although IP protection was codified in Conventions such as Berne (1886) and Paris (1896), TRIPS marks the first time that IP norms were legalized and brought under the auspices of the multilateral trade regime.

Prior to the TRIPS Agreement, the World Intellectual Property Organization (WIPO), a specialized UN agency, functioned as the global IPR administrator. Businesses in a wide range of sectors were facing substantial losses due to inadequate IP protection abroad. Indeed, Sell and Prakash estimate that US industry lost between US$43 billion and $61 billion in 1986 alone.[5] This was owing, in large part, to WIPO's blunt teeth.

Controversy over the appropriate scope and forum for IP protection has a long history.[6] However, in the early 1980s, IP-based industry forged a powerful private-sector coalition aimed at securing more stringent IP protection at both the national and international levels. In the United States, the IP-based industry successfully linked its strategic interests to the broader policy challenges plaguing the US government; this lobby was able to tap into the United States' almost obsessive focus on competitiveness and its abysmal trade deficit.[7] For the very first time, IPR was recognized as a "trade" issue.[8] The push towards heightened IPR protection and enforcement culminated in 1988 with revisions to the US Trade Act, which effectively enabled the United States Trade Representative (USTR), by invoking Section 301 of the Act, to act unilaterally against any country that failed to provide adequate protection to US-based industry.[9]

Looking beyond the United States to the Uruguay Round, the US-based Intellectual Property Committee (IPC), the UNICE, and Japan-based Keidanren joined forces shortly before its launch in September 1986 to develop a transnational private-sector consensus on IPR protection. Pharmaceutical and computer industries in particular favored a multilateral approach to securing stronger IP protection. These organizations considered it necessary to establish IPR protection standards within an international forum that had the capacity to ensure compliance. Under the leadership of the IPC, these organizations formed a trilateral coalition, the Cooperation among European, Japanese and United States Business Communities. They worked to encourage their respective governments to conclude an agreement on

IP protection in the Uruguay Round and to develop a consensus on appropriate standards for protection. Though consensus was not easily attained, the trilateral coalition produced a 100-page *Basic Framework of GATT Provisions on Intellectual Property* in the summer of 1988, calling for:

1 a code of minimum standards for copyrights, patents, trademarks, and appellation of origin issues;
2 an enforcement mechanism; and
3 a dispute settlement mechanism.[10]

It is widely agreed that the final TRIPS Agreement reflects the core priorities articulated in the *Framework*.[11]

The WTO Secretariat also played an instrumental role in the run-up to the TRIPS Agreement. Although it is conventionally understood not to play a policymaking role, the Secretariat was instrumental in the final outcome of IP negotiations by distributing the so-called "Dunkel Draft" text which mirrored the IP industry's *Framework* and, for Abbott, "provided an almost completed blueprint for the final texts adopted at Marrakesh."[12]

Intergovernmental negotiations on IP during the Uruguay Round were complex and controversial. Developing countries in particular were staunchly opposed to the inclusion of an IP code in the GATT.[13] However, in the end, they were promised a range of incentives if they agreed to a deal on IP protection including increased foreign direct investment and technology transfer.[14] IP protection was also linked to progress in other areas of particular concern to developing countries, such as agriculture and textiles. Finally, in the hope of limiting the United States' aggressive, unilateral use of Section 301 USTR, developing countries assented to moving IPR from WIPO to the multilateral trade regime. The distance between the US, Japanese, and European mandates was also initially quite wide but their positions were essentially in line with the trilateral coalition by late 1987.

The TRIPS Agreement incorporates all of the rules contained in the treaties once administered by WIPO but broadens the scope of IPR protection in important ways.[15] Most notably, most-favored-nation (MFN) and National Treatment became the basic principles underpinning the new IPR regime. The TRIPS Agreement aims to ensure that IP protection works to encourage innovation and the transfer of technology by providing a universal blueprint that sets minimum standards of protection and enforcement for each of the following: industrial property (patents, trademarks, geographic indicators of source, industrial designs), and copyright (literary and artistic works). Where patent protection is concerned, WTO members are required to provide 20-year minimum patent protection "for any [new] inventions, whether products or processes, in all fields of technology without discrimination."[16] The logic behind this provision is that the research and development (R&D) required for new inventions are costly, but cheap for generic competitors to reproduce. Granting temporary, exclusive marketing rights to the originator of a new invention allows them to charge higher prices to recoup the costs of R&D and thereby provides an incentive for new research and technological progress. This is a "low volume, high margin" strategy since it severely restricts the sale of patented goods to poor countries.

Finally, where WIPO members were free to deny patent protection at their discretion, all WTO members are required to maintain the same level of IP protection regardless of their level of development. They are required to implement minimum levels of protection for IP within their national legislation and bring their national patent regimes into line with their TRIPS obligations. Countries were, however, granted grace periods for implementing their TRIPS obligations according to their respective levels of development.[17]

The TRIPS Agreement also introduced new measures for enforcing IP rules. The shift from WIPO to TRIPS introduced the possibility of inflicting retaliatory commercial measures and, since 1995, countries can impose punitive trade sanctions in any field of trade (not just IP) on violators of the agreement. Essentially, by situating IPR inside the legal-liberal episteme, the range of policy options considered appropriate by WTO members would be constrained and the scope of future TRIPS negotiations would be limited. These developments sparked a massive backlash among NGOs, globally.

NGOs bring the Access to Medicines Campaign to the EU

In the run-up to the TRIPS Agreement in 1994, the EU adopted a hard-line, market-oriented approach to IPR protection and IP-based industry, represented by the UNICE, which was the EU's key partner on this issue. However, beginning in 1998, the Access to Medicines Campaign (Access Campaign) spread to Europe and dramatically changed the dynamics between EU policymakers and non-state actors. During this highly politicized period of policy development, NGOs became key interlocutors and, through a multi-pronged strategy, sought to compel EU policymakers working in DG Trade to initiate a ministerial declaration that would clarify TRIPS provisions on public health and guarantee governments' rights to put public health concerns above IPR protection. During the 1998–2001 period, EU policymakers responded to NGO demands by making the external trade policy-making process more transparent and open to participation. NGOs played key roles as agenda setters and educators during this phase while their demands fitted broadly within the parameters of the legal-liberal episteme.

The context 1.0

As soon as the TRIPS Agreement came into force, the United States, EU and their Pharma[18] industries took action against developing countries for *perceived* IPR violations.[19] In general, the Pharma industry was concerned that any leniency or exception made to IPR enforcement would lead to a downward erosion of IPR, leaving them unable to recover the costs of research or earn a profit on broad categories of drugs. These worries led to a series of cases against developing countries, such as South Africa and Brazil, designed to force them to uphold stringent IPR protection, even if it prevented them from addressing public health needs.

By the mid-1990s, the AIDS crisis in Africa had reached epidemic proportions; over 4.5 million people in South Africa alone had contracted HIV and many of them lacked access to affordable treatment.[20] In 1997, the South African government passed the Medicines and Related Substances Control "Amendment Act," in an effort to improve access to affordable HIV/AIDS drugs. The Act effectively allowed the government temporarily to overrule national patents by granting a compulsory license.[21] Compulsory licenses are issued by governments and allow local generic companies to produce a product, at a lower cost and for a limited time, without the patent holder's permission. Granting a compulsory license is a TRIPS-compliant option available to governments to improve access to life-saving drugs in situations of national emergency or other circumstances of extreme urgency.

Despite the apparent flexibilities in the TRIPS Agreement that allow governments to take measures to protect public health, 39 multi-national pharmaceutical companies launched a case in the High Court of South Africa against the government beginning in February 1998. They argued that the Amendment Act violated both the South African Constitution and the TRIPS Agreement. Notably, South Africa had until 2005 to bring its national patent legislation in line with its TRIPS obligations.

Although the multinational corporations in this case were weakly positioned legally, they initially received tremendous support from their national governments. In 1998, the Office of the USTR took measures to force South Africa to repeal the Act: by invoking Section 301 of the Trade Act, and by placing South Africa on its "Watch List," the USTR effectively withheld trade benefits and threatened trade sanctions if South Africa failed to repeal the Amendment Act. The EU followed suit when Sir Leon Brittan, vice-president of the European Commission, sent a veiled threat to Thabo Mbeki, vice-president of South Africa: "Section 15c of the [medicines] law in question would appear to be at variance with South Africa's obligations under the TRIPS and its implementation would negatively affect the interest of the European pharmaceutical industry."[22]

The heavy-handed tactics by Pharma and the aggressive stance taken by the United States and EU in light of the raging AIDS crisis in Africa catalyzed a coalition of AIDS activists, public health advocates, and developing countries into action. Leading NGOs, including AIDS Coalition to Unleash Power (ACT UP), Médecins Sans Frontières/ Doctors Without Borders (MSF), Health Action International (HAI), Oxfam International, Third World Network, Essential Action, Health Global Access Project, and the Consumer Project on Technology (CPTECH), launched a campaign to ensure that the TRIPS Agreement did not interfere with people's access to affordable and essential medicines.

The Access Campaign sought to establish clear links between stringent IPR enforcement and the HIV/AIDS crisis.[23] Activists disseminated information and provided research that effectively undermined the logic behind Pharma's "low volume, high margin" R&D strategy by arguing that charging high prices for medicines will not result in greater R&D for treatments for diseases that primarily afflict poor people.[24] Massive worldwide demonstrations calling for the withdrawal of the South African case publicly demonized Pharma, and US and EU officials alike. ACT UP, a key member of the Access Campaign, successfully linked the issue to Al Gore's presidential campaign. In response, the Clinton Administration withdrew its objection to the Amendment Act, both the EU and United States backed away from stringent IPR enforcement in South Africa in late 1999, and Pharma withdrew the case in May 2000.[25] It became apparent that any attempt to block access to affordable, essential medicines would endure a media firestorm, particularly in the EU and the United States.

The activism surrounding this case also highlighted broader ambiguities regarding the conditions under which WTO member state governments could provide affordable medicines for populations in emergency situations and remain TRIPS compliant.[26] First, developing countries were uncertain about the consequences of invoking these TRIPS flexibilities; they feared retaliation in the form of reduced development aid or market access if they used measures to protect public health that infringed upon the rights of powerful patent holders based in the United States and EU. Second, it appeared that developed countries and Pharma were pressuring developing countries to implement patent legislation that either went beyond their TRIPS obligations or did not account for transition periods. Third, the pharmaceutical industry argued that since:

> the spread of the HIV virus has been known since the 1980s ... this was not an emergency, but a failure of the government to prevent a predictable outcome. Private pharmaceutical companies should not therefore be forced to "pay" for a governance failure.[27]

Finally, Article 31(f) of the TRIPS Agreement specified that compulsory licenses could only be issued "predominantly for the supply of the domestic market of the Member authorizing such use." Given that most developing countries lack pharmaceutical manufacturing capabilities or have small domestic markets, only a handful of countries, such as Thailand, India, and Brazil, were legally entitled to make use of this provision. The absence of domestic pharmaceutical manufacturing capabilities remains the most significant obstacle to access to affordable medicines today.

EU engagement with the Access Campaign

By late 1999, European Commission officials realized that they would ignore the Access Campaign and the ambiguities surrounding the TRIPS Agreement at their peril.[28] In partial response to the demands of the Access Campaign, they created access points and opened up forums for consultation with NGOs working on a range of issues including public health. According to European Commission officials working in DG Trade, these new mechanisms for consultation constituted an explicit attempt to legitimize new IPR rules in the international trade regime and to co-opt NGO backlash against the TRIPS Agreement.[29]

First, members of the Access Campaign were invited to participate in a series of structured Civil Society Dialogues (CSDs) hosted by DG Trade. In part, this initiative was designed to improve transparency and public accountability of EU decision-making, especially as it pertained to the impact of TRIPS enforcement on public health. In this context,

European Commission officials met to discuss this issue together with a wide range of industry representatives, NGOs, and health advocates eight times between April 2000 and November 2001.[30] NGO participants characterize the meetings during this period as constructive opportunities to present various points of view; formal consultations evolved into a workshop format where all participants, including industry, NGOs, and Commission officials, raised issues and provided research to defend different points of view. From the perspective of NGO participants, although there was often wide disagreement, CSD meetings on TRIPS and public health fostered true dialogue during this period.[31]

Commission officials recall a less productive atmosphere in the CSD. According to the senior-level DG Trade official who was responsible for this issue and who worked closely on the negotiations leading up to the Doha Declaration, "[t]hese structured consultations became a kind of beauty contest to see who was most radical. We found out that in fact most were just there to make political statements."[32] It was a small number of well-resourced actors, including MSF and Oxfam International, that were willing to work within the existing framework of international trade rules to find solutions to the access to medicines problem and, in the view of DG Trade officials, who made constructive contributions to the dialogue. Professional NGOs with impeccable reputations, practical experience, and good moral standing were considered to be "the only ones who have the capacity to contribute real ideas and solutions, even if in the end they weren't realized."[33] Therefore, the input generated during structured, public dialogues was supplemented with informal, one-on-one meetings with a select number of NGOs including MSF and Oxfam International on a weekly basis in the period preceding the Doha Declaration.

In addition to direct consultations, members of the Access Campaign developed and distributed concrete proposals for action to EU policymakers. For example, prior to the June 2001 TRIPS Council Meeting, MSF drafted a list of recommendations for discussion and submitted it to the European Commission.[34] Members of the Access Campaign also made several submissions and directly lobbied members of the European Parliament. Although the EP lacked any formal decision-making powers at the time, the Commission consulted regularly with the Committee on International Trade during this period, and the EP passed a series of resolutions that reflect the priorities of the Access Campaign.[35]

NGOs launched a multi-pronged strategy to influence the European Commission's position on TRIPS and access to medicines. In addition

to a vibrant media campaign, NGOs were actively involved in for-
mulating policy positions and offering guidance on substantive issues
during the pre-Doha period. The consensus amongst policymakers in
the EU is that members of the Access Campaign were instrumental in
generating awareness about the public health implications of the
TRIPS Agreement. NGOs provided critical expertise, information, and
experience to which European Commission officials would not otherwise have had access. Indeed, in their absence, senior-level DG Trade
officials claimed they would have had no idea about the significance of
the AIDS crisis in the developing world or its link to IPR
enforcement.[36]

It is clear that NGOs became key interlocutors in the EU in the
period preceding the Doha Declaration; their work in the media was
instrumental in generating public debate and disseminating information about the link between IPR protection and the HIV/AIDS crisis in
Africa. While the Pharma industry enjoyed its status as a "social
partner" through its membership in the UNICE, its views were
counterbalanced by the participation of NGOs in the external trade
policymaking process. NGOs launched a sustained effort to reorient
the EU's approach to IPR enforcement in developing countries and
gave a voice to developing countries and the world's poorest people
whose interests had otherwise been marginalized in TRIPS negotiations. These NGOs enjoyed dramatically enhanced access and participatory conditions. By providing education and generating awareness
about the issue, NGOs played a decisive role in shaping and informing
the debate over the impact of the TRIPS Agreement on Access to
Medicines in the EU.

Problem solved?

The EU's position on TRIPS and public health shifted significantly
between 1998 and 2001. The EU endorsed a broad US commitment
made at the Seattle Ministerial Meeting to adjust external trade policy
to support access to HIV/AIDs drugs in Africa. In February 2001, the
EU made a further and more explicit commitment to alter its external
trade and development policies to improve access to essential medicines in developing countries. The Programme for Action to Confront
HIV/AIDS, Malaria, and Tuberculosis committed the EU to increasing the impact of existing interventions, making key pharmaceuticals
more affordable, and supporting research and development of specific
global public goods to confront these diseases.[37] The EU also became
an advocate for a global, tiered pricing system for pharmaceuticals.

At the international level, EU efforts ensured that the public health implications of IPR protection would figure prominently on the international trade agenda. The submission by the EU to the TRIPS Council in June 2001 explicitly acknowledged the freedom of all WTO members to decide the circumstances under which to grant compulsory licenses and expressed willingness to negotiate a solution to Article 31(f).[38] Subsequently, the idea of crafting a specific Doha Declaration was launched during a special informal meeting of the TRIPS Council on 25 July 2001. WTO members explicitly acknowledged that the TRIPS Agreement and its related flexibilities required clarification. The EU played the role of an honest broker, acting as a mediator between developing countries on one hand and the United States, Australia, Canada, Switzerland, and Japan on the other. Overall, the EU encouraged an interpretation of TRIPS in a manner that supported public health interests.

The Doha Declaration on the TRIPS Agreement and Public Health, adopted by the WTO Ministerial Conference on 14 November 2001, and endorsed by the EU, is widely cited as a victory for the Access Campaign.[39] This document clearly recognizes the gravity of the public health problems afflicting developing and least-developed countries (LDCs) and acknowledges that stringent IPR protection may have a negative impact on access to affordable medicines. The essence of the Declaration is contained in Article 4:

> We agree that the TRIPS Agreement does not and should not prevent members from taking measures to protect public health. Accordingly, while reiterating our commitment to the TRIPS Agreement, we affirm that the Agreement can and should be interpreted and implemented in a manner supportive of WTO members' right to protect public health and, in particular, to promote access to medicines for all.

The Declaration clarifies that all WTO member states have the right to grant compulsory licenses under any conditions they deem appropriate.[40] Members also have the right to determine what constitutes a national emergency or other circumstances of extreme urgency.[41]

Furthermore, the Declaration reconfirms members' rights to establish their own regime for exhaustion of IPR, thereby leaving the door open for parallel importation without challenge.[42] Finally, Paragraph 7 encourages developed countries to transfer technology to LDC members and iterates that LDCs are not obligated to provide patent protection to pharmaceutical products until 1 January 2016, and they may opt for an extension of the transitional period of the TRIPS Agreement until 2016.[43]

What the Doha Declaration leaves unresolved is the problem created by TRIPS Article 31(f): countries without domestic manufacturing capacity or with insufficient market demand are not permitted to make use of compulsory licenses for any purpose, including situations of national health emergencies. Instead, Paragraph 6 of the Doha Declaration recognizes this problem and commits the TRIPS Council to finding "an expeditious solution to this problem and to report to the General Council before the end of 2002."[44]

If the analysis were to stop here, as much of the existing literature that celebrates the achievements of the NGO-led Access Campaign does, we could draw optimistic conclusions about the ability of NGOs to influence EU policymakers and to affect policy outcomes by establishing and strengthening global norms to the point that even great powers cannot ignore them.[45] There are clear correlations between the demands made by members of the Access Campaign and the policy line pursued by EU policymakers in Doha. In the immediate aftermath, activists and policymakers alike celebrated the outcomes achieved in the Doha Declaration as going great distances to redress persistent inequalities in international trade rules and ensuring individual members' rights to protect public health. However, the extent to which the EU's position on public health norms actually underwent substantive and normative change is questionable, and it appears the early successes attributed to the Access Campaign were exaggerated.

With the exception of the extension of the transitory period for LDCs, the Doha Declaration clarified already existing flexibilities contained in the TRIPS Agreement.[46] Moreover, the issue of access to medicines was a deal breaker at the Ministerial Conference in Qatar; developing countries were unwilling to make concessions on a range of issues including textiles, investment, and agriculture, unless progress was made on this issue. Rather than constituting a major normative or substantive change in the global IPR regime, the Doha Declaration was merely a political compromise designed to quiet developing countries and NGOs so progress could be made in other, more crucial areas of multilateral trade negotiations. These developments worked to further the core goals of the legal-liberal episteme. A closer look at the Paragraph 6 Problem of the Doha Declaration and subsequent developments since a solution was reached reveals that early optimism regarding the Declaration's significance and the EU's "shift" in position was overstated. In many respects, the EU has fallen back to its hard-line, market-oriented approach to IPR protection, which calls into question the extent to which public health norms disseminated by NGOs involved in the Access Campaign actually took hold.

In sum, during this highly politicized stage of policy development, Commission officials responded positively to NGO demands for improved transparency and access to the external trade policymaking process in order to legitimize the legal-liberal episteme. NGOs that were willing to work within the parameters of the international trade regime to find a solution to the access to medicines issue in developing countries played crucial roles as educators and agenda setters. In response, policymakers acquiesced to NGO demands by making only incremental changes and clarifying already existing rules in the international IPR regime to maintain a forward momentum in WTO trade negotiations.

Negotiating a solution to the Paragraph 6 Problem

This section examines the role of NGOs in the development of the EU's position on solving the Paragraph 6 Problem. Between November 2002 and December 2005, this task shifted the TRIPS and public health matter from a political issue to a highly technical one in the EU. As a consequence, and despite newly created mechanisms for access and participation for non-state actors, policy discussions in the EU pulled away from the deliberative or broadly participatory process. Functional power pooled in the hands of experts and technocrats working in DG Trade and policy outcomes did not reflect the preferences of NGOs or industry. Instead, experts and technocrats were the architects of a highly complex solution, the so-called "30 August Decision" that rested soundly on liberal and legal epistemic foundations. They hope that the threat of its use, and indeed threat of competition from generic firms, will compel patent holders to sell drugs at lower costs. The effectiveness of this solution therefore depends upon competition between firms working to shift patent-holder strategies from a "high-cost, low-margin" approach to a "low-cost, high-margin" approach. Ultimately, this solution is grounded in the belief that market forces will provide equitably priced medicines and ensure research and development for infectious diseases in developing countries. Commission officials were staunch advocates of the expeditious legalization of this solution, however imperfect, and on 6 December 2005 the WTO's General Council accepted it as a permanent amendment to the TRIPS Agreement.[47] The EU subsequently passed a Regulation on 17 May 2006 implementing and giving "direct effect" to WTO General Council Decision of 30 August 2003.[48]

The context 2.0

The importance of solving the Paragraph 6 Problem was acute because the supply of low-cost, generic medicines would dry up as developing countries brought their patent legislation into line with their TRIPS obligations on 1 January 2005. Only a few developing countries have pharmaceutical manufacturing capacity, but prior to the end of the patent system moratorium for countries like India, countries were free to import generic copies of life-saving drugs such as first-line anti-retroviral treatments (ARVs).[49] In fact, by 2005, 70 percent of the HIV/AIDS treatments provided by MSF were imported from generic firms in India.[50] All new products produced after the 2005 deadline would be subject to full patent protection, but generic versions of products produced between 1995 and 2005 would still be available provided the generic producer paid royalties to the patent holder.[51] Despite these circumstances, momentum and political will declined significantly after Doha, and the TRIPS Council was unable to find a "simple and expeditious solution to this problem … before the end of 2002."[52] Moreover, the four main proposed solutions received by the TRIPS Council in 2002 indicated that a consensus would be difficult to reach.[53]

Prior to the adoption of the Doha Declaration in 2001, developing countries were already aware of the problem caused by Article 31(f) and proposed using TRIPS Article 30 as a basis for a solution to the problem.[54] This solution would allow WTO members to "give effect" to compulsory licenses issued by other members and to export pursuant to those licenses. This solution required the development of an authoritative interpretation that would allow members to "use the Article 30 exception provision to authorize production for export to address public health needs in importing Members."[55] Many developing countries maintained their preference for a limited exception clause of Article 30 in the 2002–03 period.[56] The EU even flirted with this option briefly.[57] Since this solution would result in a broad and general exception in WTO members' patent laws, it was widely viewed as the most "administratively simple, workable and economically viable" by members of the Access Campaign and the World Health Organization (WHO).[58] However, this option was eventually rejected by both the United States and the EU because it was not considered a legally secure solution and it could erode the achievements of the TRIPS Agreement.

The African Group[59] proposed a moratorium whereby WTO members would agree not to bring disputes against countries that export some medicines to countries in need.[60] The United States also initially expressed a preference for a temporary moratorium provided that it was limited to epidemics explicitly referenced in the Doha Declaration: HIV/AIDS, malaria, and tuberculosis.[61] The possibility of "waiving" certain WTO members from specific obligations under the TRIPS was also suggested by the United States as an interim solution until consensus on Paragraph 6 was attained.[62] Because both options were temporary solutions that suffered from an inherent lack of legal stability and predictability, they were eventually deemed unsustainable and inconsistent with the legal and liberal foundations of the international trade regime and therefore rejected.[63]

Another option involved carving out an exception to Article 31 of the TRIPS Agreement through an amendment. The African Group and its partners suggested that an amendment should simply delete the paragraph in Article 31(f) that limits the production of products predominantly for the domestic market. Others proposed the introduction of a limited exception that would apply only under certain circumstances "for exports of products needed to combat serious public health problems and produced under compulsory licenses."[64] Clearly, this was a much more restrictive solution than the one proposed under Article 30, and it would eventually provide the basis for the Decision of the General Council of the WTO on 30 August 2003.[65]

Initially, the EU resumed its role as an honest broker by presenting both the Articles 30 and 31 solutions as viable options[66] while struggling internally to forge a common position. Due to pressure from its sizeable pharmaceutical industry, Germany maintained a position most in-line with the United States, while many other EU members sought a much broader solution under Article 30. The UK Commission on Intellectual Property Rights also implicitly endorsed this solution by emphasizing the importance of economies of scale for generic producers.[67] There was also considerable political wrangling between different institutional arms of the EU. DG Internal Market and the patents working group of the Council of Ministers both sought restrictive solutions that would not lower intellectual property protection standards. By contrast, DG Development and the EP stood squarely behind a solution based in TRIPS Article 30.[68] In fact, on 23 October 2002, the EP passed Amendment 196 to the EU Directive 2001/83/EC relating to medicinal products for human use, officially endorsing an Article 30-based solution. Article 10, Paragraph 4 states:

> Manufacturing shall be allowed if the medicinal product is intended for export to a third country that has issued a compulsory

license for that product, or where a patent is not in force and if there is a request to that effect of the competent public health authorities of that third country.

This amendment is widely considered by NGOs to contain an "ideal solution" or blueprint for solving the Paragraph 6 Problem.

However, by June 2002, the EU and its member states were positioned squarely behind an Article 31 solution and were preoccupied with clarifying modalities. Despite considerable intergovernmental and institutional political wrangling over a range of issues—including the scope of diseases covered by the amendment, whether the exception should be limited to LDCs, which countries qualify as exporters of low-cost essential medicines, and the need for additional safeguards—the 30 August Decision was adopted in 2003.[69]

EU disengagement with the Access Campaign 1.0

Momentum for meeting with NGOs endured throughout 2002 and 2003. The CSD met three times in 2002 and four times in 2003. In each instance, the lead European Commission participant was the senior-level DG Trade official working on intellectual property, Paul Vandoren. However, by early 2003, the quality of discussion, especially as it pertained to a Paragraph 6 solution, declined significantly. As the policy debate centered on issues that required significant legal and technical know-how, discussions were "pulled back" from the participatory process. Even DG Trade's most avid and trusted NGO partners, MSF and Oxfam International, were relegated to the status of "passive receivers" of information. According to actors on both sides of the debate, CSD became one-sided "de-briefing sessions" where DG Trade officials informed attendees about their activities at the TRIPS Council and their work on modalities for implementing a solution under Article 31(f).[70] The floor was open for participants to ask one or two questions, but unlike the pre-Doha Declaration period, there was no longer any opportunity for meaningful debate. NGOs report that the sessions ended before they could advance their own point of view on the issues.[71] The intensity and quality of input were also reportedly diminished during one-on-one meetings between MSF, Oxfam International, and Commission officials. Moreover, NGO activism on the access to medicines issue began to stagnate during this period. Frustration over being sidelined in the consultative process and the hard-line market-oriented position of DG Trade officials made it difficult for NGOs to commit resources and maintain interest amongst their membership. Many turned their attention to other issues such as water services liberalization (discussed in Chapter 4).[72]

By contrast, the research-based and generic pharmaceutical industries in Europe stepped up their efforts to find an optimal solution to the Paragraph 6 Problem. The European Generics Association (EGA) endorsed an Article 30 solution in mid-2002 and advocated for the adoption of the EP's Amendment 196.[73] According to the EGA, such a solution would "facilitate the creation of economies of scale and thereby ensure the lowest possible prices for essential medicines".[74] The research-based industry lobbied aggressively against a solution based in Article 30. In the view of the European Federation of Pharmaceutical Industries and Associations (EFPIA), an Article 30 solution would go far beyond the scope of the Doha Declaration, undermine the TRIPS Agreement, and stunt progress on research and development for new drugs, particularly for diseases afflicting the world's poorest people.[75] They sought a very narrow solution based in Article 31(f) that would restrict disease scope and limit the range of countries eligible to import under the amendment to least-developed and low-income countries. In addition to attending CSD sessions, individual companies, the EGA, and the EFPIA lobbied Commission officials working on IPR in DG Internal Market and the patents working group of the Committee of Permanent Representatives. Despite these efforts, the 30 August Decision did not meet the demands of either the generic or research-based industries.

Once the EU had explicitly endorsed a solution based in Article 31(f) there was no possibility of compromise with the generic industry or NGOs working with the Access Campaign who roundly rejected such a solution. The diminishing quality of consultations in this period was largely due to overwhelming, ideological disagreements over the appropriate solution to high prices for essential medicines in developing countries. As discussed at length above, the Access Campaign attributes the high price of medicines to stringent IPR protection and therefore looked for greater flexibility in IPR enforcement vis-à-vis TRIPS Article 30. Commission officials cite a range of other problems including the failure of public policy and the lack of health infrastructure and distribution channels.[76] They also do not view compulsory licensing as a viable or sustainable solution to the access to medicines problem. Instead, they favor voluntary, market-based mechanisms. Solutions that would erode the IPR protections secured by the TRIPS agreement were simply inconceivable to European Commission officials.[77]

Incidentally, consultation between industry and DG Trade also deteriorated at this stage of policy development. Although they were a strong countervailing force to the NGO-led Access Campaign, the research-based industry was also sidelined because their proposals did not fit with the prevailing legal and liberal epistemic foundations of the international trade regime. DG Trade officials were frustrated by "their incredibly conservative and inflexible positions" that would, in practice, violate WTO rules.[78] They advanced uncompromising proposals for an Article 31 solution that would restrict disease scope, and this was something that was untenable from the point of view of DG Trade officials. Introducing such a restriction into the solution would violate one of the most fundamental principles of the international trade regime, i.e. non-discrimination, because developed countries with manufacturing capacity do not face disease limitation on the grant of compulsory licenses. Upholding this principle was deemed more important than conceding to the demands of research-based industry.[79]

Commission officials forged ahead with the 30 August Decision with the intent to maintain IPR protection and to provide legal certainty for the research-based pharmaceutical industry—two qualities that were lacking in the proposals preferred by developing countries, generic industry, NGOs, and the WHO. DG Trade experts with technical and highly specialized knowledge, were tasked with determining the modalities of an Article 31-based solution such as the precise form or limits on compulsory licensing, tiered pricing, and related safeguards against the diversion of low-priced pharmaceuticals that are intended for developing countries. They also had to devise strategies to avoid price erosion of pharmaceuticals in the markets of developed countries. They were architects of a cumbersome and bureaucratic 30 August Decision that was never expected to function in practice. Instead, the "threat" of compulsory licenses, arising from an amendment to Article 31, should lead to spontaneous price reductions as patent holders issue voluntary licenses and/or sign on to a voluntary global, tiered pricing scheme; both options are considered to be sustainable solutions to high-priced medicines and consistent with the legal and liberal foundations of the international trade regime. All NGO arguments regarding the cumbersome and complicated nature of the solution were moot from the point of view of DG Trade officials. Moreover, according to the DG Trade officials responsible for IPR at the time, they had a very small margin of maneuver to devise the solution and to ensure it did not erode the IPR protection guaranteed by the TRIPS Agreement. Therefore, it was by necessity that they pulled away from consultation with civil society and insulated the work of DG Trade from scrutiny during this phase of policy development.[80]

Problem solved ... again?

The 30 August Decision was an interim solution in the form of a waiver of Article 31(f), agreed to before the Cancun Ministerial Meeting in September 2003. It effectively allows the import of generic pharmaceuticals under compulsory license where there is insufficient manufacturing capacity on a case-by-case basis, provided that certain conditions are met.[81]

The Decision requires that importing countries (excluding LDCs)[82] notify the TRIPS Council of their general intent to make use of the system. Countries may also make a declaration of their intention not to use the system or to use it in a limited way.[83] The importing member must also provide the names of the pharmaceutical products and the quantities it expects to import, and confirm that it has insufficient or no manufacturing capacity in the sector to produce the product in question.[84] If the drug is patented in the importing country, it must grant a compulsory license in accordance with TRIPS Article 31.[85]

Exporting WTO members must also issue a compulsory license, but it must only be for the amount necessary to meet the needs of the importing member as indicated in its notification to the TRIPS Council. The TRIPS Council must also be notified by the exporting member when a compulsory license is issued, and adequate remuneration must be paid to the patent holder in the exporting country.[86] WTO members must also take reasonable measures to prevent trade diversion and re-importation of products produced and exported under this system.[87] Despite efforts by the international research-based pharmaceutical industry and the United States,[88] the Decision does not limit the scope of diseases, nor does it restrict usage to least-developed or sub-Saharan African countries.[89]

Members of the Access Campaign immediately issued widespread and unequivocal denunciations of the 30 August Decision.[90] It was (and still is) viewed as a flawed deal that is likely to make the access to essential medicines situation in developing countries far worse.[91] The system entails onerous administrative costs for developing countries with limited resources, and it is considered too complicated to work in practice.[92] For members of the Access Campaign who lobbied DG Trade officials and the EP, the burden of proof on developing countries to establish that they lack sufficient manufacturing capacity and the possibility of review by the TRIPS Council will compromise their willingness to make use of the system. This provision raises the specter of costly legal battles and/or trade retaliation in other areas for countries that apply to use the system.[93] Moreover, the precise meaning of "insufficient capacity" is unclear and therefore subject to dispute. NGOs have also taken issue with the fact that potential importers under this system are entirely dependent upon government decisions in exporting countries.[94]

For the Access Campaign, an energetic market in developing countries for generic medicines is essential to combat AIDS and other public health problems. However, NGOs believe the Decision makes it difficult for generic producers to establish viable economies of scale that will drive the price of essential medicines down.[95] Moreover, there is concern that in the absence of competition, Indian and Brazilian generic industries will be predatory in their pricing practices. The system does not allow for international tendering, and the requirement for double licensing (in both the importing and exporting countries) adds an unnecessary layer of bureaucracy and uncertainty for generic producers. Because they may only produce products for export on a case-by-case, license-by-license basis, prospective generic producers may be deterred from building up capacity for export on speculation. NGOs are also concerned that the requirement for distinctive labeling to prevent trade diversion and the payment of remuneration in wealthy OECD countries will drive generic prices upwards.[96] The generic industry has echoed many of these concerns, particularly the EGA, which considers the system so constraining and legally risky that it will not make use of it.[97] The Decision also failed to meet the expectations of the international research-based industry. Pharma was especially frustrated by the decision not to include limits on the scope of diseases but was appeased by the declarations of non-use by a wide range of countries.[98]

EU disengagement with the Access Campaign 2.0

After August 2003, policy discussions focused on finding a permanent solution to the Paragraph 6 Problem and the issue became even more complex and technical. As a result, additional functional power pooled in the hands of DG Trade officials who sought to make use of their carefully crafted 30 August Decision as an authoritative basis for a new and permanent rule on compulsory licensing in countries with no manufacturing capacity. According to DG Trade officials, they were committed to ensuring that the solution to the Paragraph 6 Problem rested on sound liberal and legal epistemic foundations: "[w]e were and always have been in favor of a sustainable and legally secure fix. A waiver is by nature temporary. We wanted a permanent, market-based fix."[99]

The quality of engagement between European Commission officials and NGOs working with the Access Campaign degenerated further during this period. While they once served as key interlocutors in the TRIPS and access to medicines debate in the EU's external trade policymaking process, DG Trade officials questioned whether public health advocates and NGOs even qualified as stakeholders in the post-August 2003 policymaking environment. Indeed, DG Trade officials claimed that once the 30 August Decision was made, NGO proposals were increasingly incomprehensible to them during this period.[100] Only two formal CSDs were held between September 2003 and December 2005. In previous years, the head of the DG Trade unit responsible for IP was the lead participant in dialogues on TRIPS and public health with civil society; following the 30 August Decision, low-level administrators from DG Trade attended the meetings in a "debriefing" capacity. Regular, informal contact was maintained with MSF and Oxfam International, but these sessions were said to be frustrating and unproductive in the absence of any possibility of compromise.[101]

NGOs reported difficulty in maintaining momentum and interest in their campaign. They were at a distinct disadvantage in the policymaking process because of the highly technical nature of policy discussions. It was difficult to develop sufficient technical and legal expertise amongst membership to engage in substantive debates about modalities.[102] Therefore, members of the Access Campaign focused their efforts on more general public statements and position papers calling for developing countries to resist EU and US pressure to translate the 30 August Decision into a permanent TRIPS Amendment.[103] NGOs also targeted MEPs, calling on them to encourage research and development for neglected diseases and to address US-initiated free trade agreements (FTAs) that require signatories to implement and enforce more stringent IPR protection than is required by the TRIPS Agreement.[104]

In intergovernmental negotiations, a legal debate ensued over how, or indeed whether, to incorporate the 30 August Decision into the TRIPS Agreement. In two separate filings with the TRIPS Council, the EU[105] and the United States[106] took the position that it was just a technical matter of incorporating the Decision into the TRIPS Agreement.

However, the African Group, strongly supported by NGOs, was reluctant to make a solution permanent which was, in its view, complicated, untested in practice, and reached under duress prior to the Cancun Ministerial Meeting. Instead, the African Group took the view that negotiations on finding a lasting and satisfactory solution would continue during the amendment process. In 2004, it proposed dropping many of the safeguards and procedural requirements of the Decision, including those concerning notification and trade diversion, and adding a second sub-paragraph for when Article 31(f) did not apply.[107] Despite the strong stance taken by the African Group, many other developing countries were suffering from negotiation fatigue and were less hopeful that better terms could be achieved in the amendment process. Thus a split emerged between developing countries over how to proceed.

Against the backdrop of resistance from members of the Access Campaign and the growing disunity amongst developing countries, WTO members agreed to translate the 30 August Decision into the TRIPS Agreement by adding a formal amendment, Article 31*bis*[108] at the Hong Kong Ministerial Meeting in 2005.[109] The amendment does not take effect or become enforceable until it is ratified by at least two-thirds of WTO membership.[110] In the meantime, countries will continue to rely on the 30 August Decision. Since the substantive aspects of the decisions are identical, this distinction has little significance in practice. Nonetheless, in the absence of concrete evidence that the system will work to effectively meet global needs for affordable generic medicines, NGOs and public health advocates encouraged WTO members not to ratify the amendment. The original deadline for ratification was December 2007, but this was extended to the end of 2015.[111]

Before ratifying the amendment, steps were taken to create a legal basis in the EU for granting compulsory licenses for export. On 17 May 2006, the EP and the Council adopted Regulation No. 816/2006 on compulsory licensing of patents relating to the manufacture of pharmaceutical products for export to countries with public health problems.[112] This regulation effectively brought the EU member states' patent regimes into line with the 30 August Decision. On 24 October 2007, the EU officially ratified the TRIPS Amendment[113] and effectively pushed the Access Campaign in Europe back into the streets and the media.[114]

Overall, experts and technocrats in DG Trade were empowered at this stage of policy development, relative to NGOs and industry, to develop new rules in a complex issue area that required use of their specialized knowledge to find a market-based, legalized solution to the Paragraph 6 Problem. They also served as gatekeepers by determining who had a voice in the EU's external trade policymaking process. Where NGO and industry demands were inconsistent with the legal and liberal epistemic foundations of the international trade regime, their proposals were inconceivable to Commission officials as solutions to the Paragraph 6 Problem, and they were effectively sidelined in the consultative process. At the same time, DG Trade officials pulled back from the CSD and informal one-on-one meetings with industry and NGOs in order to devise modalities for a solution based in TRIPS Article 31. As the primary architects of the 30 August Decision, their policy prescriptions served as the basis for the TRIPS Amendment Concerning Article 31*bis*.

Conclusion

This chapter examined whether the increasing role of NGOs in the EU's external trade policymaking process has an impact on trade processes and policy outcomes by revisiting a case that has been celebrated as indicative of the potential of NGOs to promote social justice—the Access to Medicines Campaign. The evidence shows that the impact of NGOs on trade policy outcomes in this area has been limited. Despite early optimism, the EU's position on access to medicines did not undergo substantive, normative changes as a result of NGO advocacy, nor did the Doha Declaration signal the triumph of public health norms over stringent IPR protection. This is owing to the robust legal and liberal epistemic foundations of the international trade regime that structured patterns of empowerment in three distinct ways.

First, the imperative to legitimize the shift from GATT to WTO and to deflect criticism about the expanded scope of international trade rules led policymakers in the EU to respond positively to NGO demands for a voice in the external trade policymaking process. In the access to medicines case, this allowed NGOs that were willing to work within the WTO framework to become important interlocutors, educating both the public and policymakers about the links between stringent IPR enforcement and the HIV/AIDS crisis in Africa and giving a voice to otherwise marginalized people in the international trade regime.

Second, tensions are created between epistemes and NGOs when claims to democracy, sustainability, and justice conflict with widely held norms, consensual scientific knowledge, and ideological beliefs that underpin the prevailing episteme. EU policymakers attempted to maintain forward momentum in international trade negotiations and to co-opt NGOs in the Access Campaign by agreeing to the Doha Declaration in 2001. However, the debate over appropriate solutions to the Paragraph 6 Problem revealed deep ideological cleavages between DG Trade officials and NGOs. The former are convinced that market-based forces that uphold stringent IPR protection are sufficient to overcome the Paragraph 6 Problem, provide equitably priced medicines to countries lacking sufficient manufacturing capacity, and ensure research and development for infectious diseases in developing countries. By contrast, NGOs believe that relaxing IPR protection is essential to ensuring equitable access to affordable medicines, a policy line that is both inconceivable to DG Trade officials and challenges the legal and liberal epistemic foundations of the international trade regime. These tensions have proven to be irreconcilable.

Third, technocrats and experts are empowered, relative to other actors, to maintain and reinforce the episteme. Where policy discussions concern highly technical or complex problems, such as the Paragraph 6 Problem, technocrats serve as gatekeepers in the policymaking process. The precise role of both NGOs and industry in the access to medicines case was determined by the fitness of their demands with the prevailing legal-liberal episteme. Once NGOs and the generic industry issued wholesale rejections of an Article 31-based solution to the Paragraph 6 Problem, they were sidelined in the EU's external trade policymaking process. Similarly, consultations between DG Trade officials and research-based industry were reduced once industry became staunch advocates for the erosion of non-discrimination in international trade rules by introducing limitations on disease scope into the Paragraph 6 solution. Moreover, by virtue of their specialized knowledge, technocrats and experts are empowered to make authoritative interpretations of the rules and to develop new rules in highly technical areas. Once the decision had been made to pursue an Article 31-based solution to Paragraph 6, DG Trade officials retreated from broadly participatory processes in order to insulate their work from public scrutiny and to devise modalities for such a solution. They were the main architects of the 30 August Decision and, eventually, the TRIPS Amendment Concerning Article 31*bis*, a solution so fraught with bureaucratic red tape, it has scarcely been used in practice. Indeed, it was expected by EU policymakers that the mere threat of its use would compel patent holders to sell drugs at lower costs and shift their marketing strategies from a "low-volume, high-margin" approach to a "high-volume, low-margin" approach—something that has not occurred to date. Meanwhile, developed countries, led by the EU and United States, push poor countries to sign on to TRIPS-plus measures in FTAs, standards of patent protection and enforcement that go well beyond those of the TRIPS Agreement and that will, in effect, reduce the flexibilities secured in the Doha Declaration.

In sum, this chapter shows that NGOs are likely to improve the procedural legitimacy of policymaking when they are formally integrated into governance processes through participatory and access mechanisms. However, their ability to affect the output of policy is clearly limited. The next chapter turns to a case where NGO advocacy took place on the margins of the governing arrangements and played out in the streets and in the media rather than through formal participatory mechanisms established by the EU.

Notes

1 This chapter draws on Erin Hannah, "NGOs and the European Union: Examining the Power of Epistemes in the EC's TRIPS and Access to Medicines Negotiations," *Journal of Civil Society* 7, no. 2 (2011): 179–206. The author kindly thanks Taylor & Francis for allowing it to be reproduced here.

2 Susan K. Sell and Aseem Prakash, "Using Ideas Strategically: The Contest Between Business and NGO Networks in Intellectual Property Rights," *International Studies Quarterly* 48, no. 1 (2004): 143–175. For an examination of the role of NGOs in shaping developing country positions on the access to medicines issue see Duncan Matthews, *Intellectual Property Rights, Human Rights and Development: The Role of NGOs and Social Movements* (Northampton, Mass.: Edward Elgar, 2012).

3 The findings in Chapters 3 and 4 are based on semi-structured elite interviews with NGO officials, industry officials, permanent member state representatives, members of the EESC, officials working in the Secretariat General, DG Trade, and DG Market.

4 Susan Sell, *Private Power, Public Law: The Globalization of Intellectual Property Rights* (Cambridge: Cambridge University Press, 2003); Susan Sell and Christopher May, *Intellectual Property Rights: A Critical History* (Boulder, Colo.: Lynne Reiner Publishers, 2005); and Duncan Matthews, *Globalizing Intellectual Property: The TRIPS Agreement* (Abingdon: Routledge, 2002).

5 Sell and Prakash, "Using Ideas Strategically," 143–175, 154.

6 See Susan Sell and Christopher May, *Intellectual Property Rights: A Critical History* (Boulder, Colo.: Lynne Rienner, 2006).

7 Sell and Prakash, "Using Ideas Strategically," 156.

8 The Reagan Administration pursued a trade policy aimed at restoring US international competitiveness by restructuring and in many cases establishing intellectual property rights systems in developing countries. These priorities are reflected in the so-called "Young Report," as well as the "President's Trade Policy Action Plan (TPAP)" of 1985.

9 Sell and Prakash, "Using Ideas Strategically," 156.

10 Ibid., 159.

11 Frederick M. Abbott, "The Doha Declaration on the TRIPS Agreement and Public Health: Lighting a Dark Corner at the WTO," *Journal of International Economic Law* 5, no. 2 (2002): 469–505.

12 Abbott, "The Doha Declaration on the TRIPS Agreement and Public Health," 477.

13 J.P. Singh, "The Evolution of National Interests: New Issues and North-South Negotiations During the Uruguay Round," in *Negotiating Trade: Developing Countries in the WTO and NAFTA*, ed. John S. Odell (Cambridge: Cambridge University Press, 2006), 61–63.

14 Keith E. Maskus, "The Role of Intellectual Property Rights in Encouraging Foreign Direct Investment and Technology Transfer," *Duke Journal of Comparative and International Law* 9 no. 1 (1999): 109–161.

15 Notably, the TRIPS Agreement has been commonly referred to as a Berne and Paris-Plus Agreement.

16 WTO, "Marrakesh Agreement Establishing the World Trade Organization, Annex 1C—Agreement on Trade-Related Aspects of Intellectual Property," Article 27.1, Morocco, 15 April 1994, www.wto.org/english/docs_e/legal_e/27-trips_01_e.htm.

17 See Article 66.1, TRIPS Agreement; and WTO, "Responding to Least Developed Countries' Special Needs in Intellectual Property," 16 October 2013, www.wto.org/english/tratop_e/trips_e/ldc_e.htm.

18 This is a common reference to major research-based pharmaceutical enterprises operating on a global scale. It should be distinguished from PhRMA, a US-based pharmaceutical industry lobby organization.

19 Emanuel Adler and Steven Bernstein, "Knowledge in Power: The Epistemic Construction of Global Governance," in *Power and Global Governance*, ed. Michael Barnett and Raymond Duvall (Cambridge: Cambridge University Press, 2005), 294–318.

20 Ellen 't Hoen, "TRIPS, Pharmaceutical Patents and Access to Essential Medicines," *Chicago Journal of International Law* 3, no. 1 (2002): 27–46.

21 David Barnard, "In the High Court of South Africa, Case No. 4138/98: The Global Politics of Access to Low-cost AIDS Drugs in Poor Countries," *Kennedy Institute of Ethics Journal* 12, no. 2 (2002): 159–174.

22 Quoted in 't Hoen, "TRIPS," 27–46.

23 Sell and Prakash, "Using Ideas Strategically," 143–175; 't Hoen, "TRIPS," 27–46; and Médecins Sans Frontières (MSF), *Amsterdam Statement to WTO Member States on Access to Medicines*, 26 November 1999, www.haiweb.org/campaign/novseminar/amsterdam_statement.html.

24 Frederick M. Abbott, "The Doha Declaration on the TRIPS Agreement and Public Health: Lighting a Dark Corner at the WTO," *Journal of International Economic Law* 5, no. 2 (2002): 469–505.

25 Sell and Prakash, "Using Ideas Strategically," 165.

26 European Communities, "Programme for Action: Accelerated Action on HIV/AIDS, Malaria, and Tuberculosis in the Context of Poverty Reduction,"*Communication from the Commission to the Council and the European Parliament* (COM[2001] 96 Final), 2001.

27 Stine Jessen Haakonsson and Lisa Ann Richey, "TRIPS and Public Health: The Doha Declaration and Africa," *Development Policy Review* 25, no. 1 (2007): 75.

28 Interview with Jean-Charles Van Eeckhaute, DG Trade Commission Official, formerly (September 2000–June 2004) responsible for the international aspects of intellectual property, Brussels, Belgium, 10 February 2006.

29 Interview with Sabine Weyand, DG Trade Commission Official, former member of Pascal Lamy's Cabinet responsible for relations with the European Parliament, Social Partners and NGOs, Brussels, Belgium, 2 June 2005.

30 For a list of CSD meetings and participants see trade.ec.europa.eu/civil soc/meeting_archive.cfm#_year-2000 and trade.ec.europa.eu/civilsoc/m eeting_archive.cfm#_year-2001. For a sense of the discussions taking place in the CSD during this period see trade.ec.europa.eu/doclib/docs/ 2005/april/tradoc_122197.pdf.

31 Interview with Seco Gerard, MSF Access Campaign: EU Liaison Officer, Brussels, Belgium, 9 February 2006.

32 Interview with Jean-Charles Van Eeckhaute, DG Trade Commission Official formerly (September 2000–June 2004) in charge of international aspects of intellectual property, Brussels, Belgium, 10 February 2006.

33 Interview with Jean-Charles Van Eeckhaute, DG Trade Commission Official formerly (September 2000–June 2004) in charge of international aspects of intellectual property, Brussels, Belgium, 10 February 2006.

34 MSF, "Recommendations to the European Commission for Discussions at the June 2001 TRIPS Council on Health and Access to Medicines," 2001, www.msfaccess.org/content/recommendations-european-commission-discussions-june-2001-trips-council-health-and-access.

35 "European Parliament Resolution on Access to Drugs for HIV/AIDS Victims in the Third World, Text adopted by the European Parliament," *Official Journal of the European Communities* (European Parliament C 343/301), 15 March 2001.

36 Interview with Sabine Weyand, DG Trade Commission Official, former member of Pascal Lamy's Cabinet responsible for relations with the European Parliament, Social Partners and NGOs, Brussels, Belgium, 2 June 2005.

37 European Communities, "Programme for Action."

38 WTO, "The Relationship Between the Provisions of the TRIPS Agreement and Access to Medicines," Communication from the European Communities and their Member States to Council for TRIPS (Council for Trade-Related Aspects of Intellectual Property Rights [Council for TRIPS] IP/C/W/280), 20 June 2001. The EU did maintain an industry-oriented, hard-line approach to Article 30 exceptions and data protection. However, the significance of this became clear only when solutions to the Paragraph 6 Problem were being discussed.

39 WTO, "Doha Declaration on the TRIPS Agreement and Public Health" (WT/MIN[01]/DEC/2), 14 November 2001.

40 WTO, "Doha Declaration," Paragraph 5b.

41 WTO, "Doha Declaration," Paragraph 5c. This principle is in stark contrast to the United States' preferred outcome which would have established an exhaustive list of "qualifying" diseases. "Contribution from Australia, Canada, Japan, Switzerland, and the United States, Preambular Language for Ministerial Declaration: Access to Medicines for HIV/AIDS and Other Pandemics" (Council for TRIPS IP/C/W/313), 4 October 2001.

42 WTO, "Doha Declaration," Paragraph 5d.

43 This decision was formalized by the TRIPS Council in 2002. In 2005, the TRIPS Council decided that LDCs would not have to comply with the TRIPS Agreement in general (not just as it pertains to pharmaceuticals) until 2013. Articles 3, 4, and 5 were the exceptions and LDCs could not "roll back" their TRIPS compliance. In July 2013, at the request of the LDC Group, the TRIPS Council extended the transition period again to 1 July 2021. See South Centre, "South Centre Welcomes WTO Decision on LDCs and TRIPS," *South Bulletin* 74 (July 2013), www.southcentre. int/question/south-centre-welcomes-wto-decision-on-ldcs-and-trips/.

44 Abbott, "The Doha Declaration," 469–505.

45 Sell and Prakash, "Using Ideas Strategically," 167.

46 Notably, most African countries have already brought national patent legislation into line with the TRIPS Agreement.

47 WTO, "Amendment of the TRIPS Agreement" (WT/L/641), 8 December 2005.

48 European Communities, "Regulation (EC) No. 816/2006 of the European Parliament and of the Council of 17 May 2006 on Compulsory Licensing of Patents Relating to the Manufacture of Pharmaceutical Products for Export to Countries with Public Health Problems," *Official Journal of the European Communities* (L157/1), 2006.

49 Faizel Ismail, "The Doha Declaration on TRIPS and Public Health and the Negotiations in the WTO on Paragraph 6: Why PhRMA Needs to Join the Consensus!," *Journal of World Intellectual Property* 6, no. 3 (2003): 394–401.

50 MSF, "Prognosis: Short-term Relief, Long-term Pain: The Future of Generic Medicines Made in India," 2005, www.doctorswithoutborders. org/article/prognosis-short-term-relief-long-term-pain.

51 Haakonsson and Richey, "TRIPS and Public Health," 79.

52 WTO, "Doha Declaration on the TRIPS Agreement and Public Health" (WT/MIN[01]/DEC/2), 14 November 2001.

53 Duncan Matthews, "WTO Decision on Implementation of Paragraph 6 of the Doha Declaration on the TRIPS Agreement and Public Health: A Solution to the Access to Essential Medicines Problem?," *Journal of International Economic Law* 7, no. 1 (2004): 73–107.

54 WTO, "Proposal by African Group, Bangladesh, Barbados, Bolivia, Brazil, Cuba, Dominican Republic, Ecuador, Haiti, Honduras, India, Indonesia, Jamaica, Pakistan, Paraguay, Philippines, Peru, Sri Lanka, Thailand and Venezuela, Ministerial Declaration of the TRIPS Agreement and Public Health" (Council for TRIPS IP/C/W/312 WT/GC/W/450), 4 October 2001.

55 Frederick M. Abbott and Jerome H. Reichman, "Access to Essential Medicines: Lessons Learned since the Doha Declaration on the TRIPS Agreement and Public Health, and Policy Options for the European Union," Study Commissioned by the European Parliament's Committee on International Trade (Brussels: European Parliament, 2007), 6.

56 WTO, "Paragraph 6 of the Doha Declaration of the TRIPS Agreement and Public Health, Communication from the Permanent Mission of Brazil on behalf of the delegations of Bolivia, Brazil, Cuba, China, Dominican Republic, Ecuador, India, Indonesia, Pakistan, Peru, Sri

Lanka, Thailand and Venezuela" (Council for TRIPS IP/C/W/355), 24 June 2002.

57 WTO, "Paragraph 6 of the Doha Declaration of the TRIPS Agreement and Public Health, Communication from the European Communities and their Member States" (Council for TRIPS IP/C/W/352), 12 March 2002.

58 't Hoen, "TRIPS," 59.

59 The African Group is composed of the 42 African members of the WTO. For a list of members, see www.wto.org/english/tratop_e/dda_e/negotia ting_groups_e.htm#grp002.

60 WTO, "Proposal on Paragraph 6 of the Doha Declaration on the TRIPS Agreement on Public Health, Joint Communication from the African Group in the WTO" (Council for TRIPS IP/C/W/351), 24 June 2002.

61 WTO, "Paragraph 6 of the Doha Declaration of the TRIPS Agreement and Public Health, Communication from the United States" (Council for TRIPS IP/C/W/358), 9 July 2002; Ismail, "The Doha Declaration on TRIPS," 399.

62 Jacques H.J. Bourgeois and Thaddeus J. Burns, "Implementing Paragraph 6 of the Doha Declaration on TRIPS and Public Health: The Waiver Solution," *Journal of World Intellectual Property* 5, no. 6 (2002): 835–864; Paul Vandoren and Jean Charles Van Eeckhaute, "The WTO Decision on Paragraph 6 of the Doha Declaration on the TRIPS Agreement and Public Health: Making it Work," *Journal of World Intellectual Property* 6, no. 6 (2003): 779–793.

63 Matthews, "WTO Decision," 85.

64 WTO, "Paragraph 6 of the Doha Declaration of the TRIPS Agreement and Public Health, Communication from the European Communities and their Member States" (Council for TRIPS IP/C/W/352), 12 March 2002.

65 WTO, "Implementation of Paragraph 6 of the Doha Declaration on the TRIPS Agreement and Public Health" (General Council WT/L/540 and Corr.1), 30 August 2003.

66 WTO, "Concept Paper Relating to Paragraph 6 of the Doha Declaration on the TRIPS Agreement and Public Health, Communication from the European Communities and their Member States" (Council for TRIPS IP/C/W/339), 2002.

67 United Kingdom Commission on Intellectual Property Rights, "Integrating Intellectual Property Rights and Development Policy," Final Report, 2002, 44–48, www.iprcommission.org/graphic/documents/final_ report.htm.

68 The European Parliament's position was in line with the Access Campaign throughout subsequent stages of policy development. See "European Parliament Resolution on HIV/AIDS: Time to Deliver," European Parliament resolution P6_TA(2006)0321, 6 July 2006; "European Parliament Resolution on AIDS," European Parliament resolution P6_TA (2006)0526, 30 November 2006; "European Parliament Resolution on the TRIPS Agreement and Access to Medicines," European Parliament resolution P6_TA-PROV(2007)0353, 12 July 2007.

69 Frederick M. Abbott, "The WTO Medicines Decision: World Pharmaceutical Trade and the Protection of Public Health," *American Journal of*

International Law 99, no. 2 (2005): 317–358; Matthews, "WTO Decision," 73–107.

70 Confidential interview with DG Trade official working on New Technologies, Intellectual Property and Public Procurement, Brussels, Belgium, 2 February 2006; interview with Seco Gerard, MSF Access Campaign: EU Liaison Officer, Brussels, Belgium, 5 June 2005.

71 Interview with Louis Belanger, Oxfam International: EU Advocacy and Media Officer, Brussels, Belgium, 8 February 2006.

72 Interview with Marc Maes, European Policy Officer, Coalition of the Flemish North-South Movement 11.11.11, Brussels, Belgium, 6 June 2005.

73 EGA, "Outcome of the WTO Ministerial Conference, Doha Declaration on the TRIPS and Public Health," Position Paper, February 2002; EGA, "Generic Medicines Producers Back Measure to Help Stimulate Access to Medicines in Least Developed Countries," *EGA Press Release*, 9 December 2002.

74 EGA, "Generic Medicines Producers Back Measure," Press Release, 9 December 2002, 198.170.119.137/pr-2002-12-09.htm.

75 CEOs of international research-based pharmaceutical companies (including those based in Europe) outlined their preferred solution to the Paragraph 6 Problem in a "Comprehensive Strategy on Access to Medicines in the Poorest Countries," www.cptech.org/ip/wto/p6/8.pdf. Pharma also outlined the principles underpinning its position on the issue in two letters in mid-2003 to USTR Robert B. Zoellick, www.cptech.org/ip/wto/p6/1.pdf and www.cptech.org/ip/wto/p6/5.pdf.

76 Confidential interview with DG Trade official working on New Technologies, Intellectual Property and Public Procurement, Brussels, Belgium, 13 February 2006.

77 Confidential interview with DG Trade official working on New Technologies, Intellectual Property and Public Procurement, Brussels, Belgium, 13 February 2006.

78 Interview with Jean-Charles Van Eeckhaute, DG Trade Commission Official formerly (September 2000–June 2004) in charge of international aspects of intellectual property, Brussels, Belgium, 10 February 2006.

79 Confidential interview with DG Trade official working on New Technologies, Intellectual Property and Public Procurement, Brussels, Belgium, 2 February 2006.

80 The findings in this paragraph are based on two confidential interviews with DG Trade officials working on New Technologies, Intellectual Property and Public Procurement, Brussels, Belgium, 2 and 13 February 2006.

81 Abbott and Reichman, *Access to Essential Medicines.*

82 LDCs are exempt from this requirement since they are assumed to lack the manufacturing capacity to produce pharmaceuticals and are thus already eligible to use the system.

83 Most OECD countries and all EU member states including newly acceded countries have made such a declaration.

84 WTO, "Implementation of Paragraph 6 of the Doha Declaration on the TRIPS Agreement and Public Health" (General Council WT/L/540 and Corr.1), 30 August 2003, Paragraph 2(a)ii, Annex.

85 WTO, "Implementation of Paragraph 6 of the Doha Declaration on the TRIPS Agreement and Public Health," *Paragraph 2(a)iii.*

86 WTO, "Implementation of Paragraph 6 of the Doha Declaration on the TRIPS Agreement and Public Health," *Paragraph 3.*

87 WTO, "Implementation of Paragraph 6 of the Doha Declaration on the TRIPS Agreement and Public Health," *Paragraph 4.*

88 Ismail, "The Doha Declaration on TRIPS," 398.

89 WTO, "Implementation of Paragraph 6 of the Doha Declaration on the TRIPS Agreement and Public Health."

90 CPTech posted press releases, letters, and position papers from various NGOs expressing this sentiment during the 2003–05 period. See www.cp tech.org/ip/wto/p6/.

91 Interview with Louis Belanger, EU Advocacy and Media Officer, Oxfam International, Brussels, Belgium, 8 February 2006.

92 As of June 2015, only Rwanda has notified the TRIPS Council of its intent to use the system by importing 260,000 packs of "Apo-TriAvir," a combination HIV/AIDS drug from Canada. It took nearly three years for only two shipments of ARVs to be sent to Rwanda under Canada's Access to Medicines Regimes. Notably, Apotex, the generic firm that won the tender to manufacture and export the drug to Rwanda, says it will never participate in such an arrangement again because the procedure was so cumbersome and consumed so many company resources. See Apotex, "Canada's Access to Medicines Regime Must Be Fixed," press release, March 2011 at www.apotex.com/apotriavir/. See also International Center for Trade and Sustainable Development, "Canadian WTO Notification Clears Path for Rwanda to Import Generic HIV/AIDS Drug," *Bridges Weekly Trade News Digest* 11, no. 34, 10 October 2007.

93 Interview with Seco Gerard, MSF Access Campaign: EU Liaison Officer, Brussels, Belgium, 9 February 2006.

94 Interview with Jennifer Brant, International Trade Analyst at Sidley Austin LLP and former Trade Policy Advisor with Oxfam America, Geneva, Switzerland, 24 February 2006.

95 Interview with Seco Gerard, MSF Access Campaign: EU Liaison Officer, Brussels, Belgium, 9 February 2006.

96 Interview with Jennifer Brant, International Trade Analyst at Sidley Austin LLP and former Trade Policy Advisor with Oxfam America, Geneva, Switzerland, 24 February 2006.

97 EGA, "Proposal for a Regulation of the European Parliament and of the Council on Compulsory Licensing of Patents Relating to the Manufacture of Pharmaceutical Products for Export to Countries with Public Health Problems," Position Paper, March 2005.

98 Interview with Adrien Van den Hoven, Director of the International Relations Department and WTO Advisor, UNICE, Brussels, Belgium, 24 September 2004.

99 Confidential interview with DG Trade official working on New Technologies, Intellectual Property and Public Procurement, Brussels, Belgium, 2 February 2006.

100 Confidential interview with DG Trade official working on New Technologies, Intellectual Property and Public Procurement, Brussels, Belgium, 2 February 2006.

101 Interview with Seco Gerard, MSF Access Campaign: EU Liaison Officer, Brussels, Belgium, 9 February 2006; Confidential interview with DG Trade official working on New Technologies, Intellectual Property and Public Procurement, Brussels, Belgium, 13 February 2006.

102 Interview with Seco Gerard, MSF Access Campaign: EU Liaison Officer, Brussels, Belgium, 9 February 2006.

103 See, for example, this joint NGO statement released 3 December 2005, by the Consumer Project on Technology, "WTO Members Should Reject Bad Deal on Medicines, Joint Statement by NGOs on TRIPS and Public Health," www.cptech.org/ip/wto/p6/ngos12032005.html.

104 Ellen 't Hoen, *The Global Politics of Pharmaceutical Monopoly Power: Drug Patents, Access, Innovation, and the Application of the WTO Doha Declaration on TRIPS and Public Health* (Diemen, Netherlands: AMB Publishers, 2009).

105 "Implementation of the General Council Decision on Paragraph 6 of the Doha Declaration on the TRIPS Agreement and Public Health, Communication from the European Communities" (Council for TRIPS IP/C/W/416), 17 November 2003.

106 WTO, "Comments on the Implementation of the 30 August 2003 Agreement (Solution) on the TRIPS Agreement and Public Health, Communication from the United States" (Council for TRIPS IP/C/W/444), 18 March 2005.

107 Implementation of Paragraph 11 of the 30 August 2003 Decision, Communication from Nigeria on Behalf of the African Group (Council for TRIPS IP/C/W/437), 10 December 2004.

108 "*bis*" refers to an addition to an existing Article. In this case, it refers to an addition to TRIPS Article 31.

109 WTO, "Amendment of the TRIPS Agreement: Decision of 6 December 2005," WT/L/6418 December 2005.

110 As of June 2015, 54 WTO members (including 27 members of the EU) have ratified the Amendment. Members accepting the amendment of the TRIPS Agreement can be found at: www.wto.org/english/tratop_e/trips_e/amendment_e.htm.

111 WTO, "Amendment of the TRIPS Agreement—Fourth Extension of the Period for the Acceptance by Members of the Protocol Amending the TRIPS Agreement," WT/L/899, 26 November 2013.

112 "Regulation (EC) No. 816/2006 of the European Parliament and of the Council of 17 May 2006 on Compulsory Licensing of Patents Relating to the Manufacture of Pharmaceutical Products for Export to Countries with Public Health Problems," *Official Journal of the European Communities* (European Communities L157/1), 2006.

113 "European Parliament Legislative Resolution on the Proposal for a Council Decision on the Acceptance, on behalf of the European Community, the Protocol Amending the TRIPS Agreement, done at Geneva on 6 December 2005," European Parliament resolution P6_ TA-PROV (2007)0459, 24 October 2007.

114 The focus of Access activism has shifted away from the TRIPS Amendment to the EU's efforts to enforce more stringent IP protection than is required by the TRIPS Agreement in its bilateral and regional FTAs. MSF, for example, launched a new campaign entitled, "Europe! Hands

Off Our Medicine" in October 2010. The campaign targets TRIPS-Plus provisions currently being negotiated by the EU in FTAs, the EU practice of exerting bilateral pressure to prevent developing countries from invoking TRIPS flexibilities, and seizure of generic medicines in transit in Europe and en route to developing countries. This campaign relies almost exclusively on media-based activism. See www.msfaccess.org/ma in/access-patents/hands-off-our-medicine-campaign/.

4 Too thirsty to keep fighting?
NGOs and the EU's quest for water services liberalization

- Locking services liberalization into the multilateral trade regime
- NGO backlash to the GATS: spotlight on water services liberalization
- Secrets, leaks, and the launch of a campaign
- Request, react, rejoice?
- Conclusion

With the conclusion of the 1994 General Agreement of Trade in Services (GATS), WTO members shifted services from traditional, national regulatory regimes to multilateral, market-based rules embodied in the international trade regime. This move would entrench services within the legal-liberal episteme, define what policy options would be conceivable in subsequent negotiations, and engender massive blowback from NGOs.

The EU's requests for water services liberalization, particularly water for human use—the collection, purification, and distribution of natural water—in developing and least-developed countries, sparked widespread outrage and condemnation, especially among NGOs.[1] At the heart of this reaction is the fundamental belief that liberalizing water services and opening up water markets to foreign competition constitute full frontal attacks on democracy and basic human rights.[2] NGOs working on this issue fundamentally reject the entrenchment of services in the multilateral trade regime and consider a full-scale moratorium on GATS negotiations the only acceptable outcome of their advocacy.[3] Early on it became clear to NGOs and EU policymakers alike that neither compromise nor co-optation was possible in this case. Given the intractability of the situation, and in contrast to NGOs working on the access to medicines issue, groups mobilized from outside the EU's formal political process to pursue an aggressive, multipronged protest campaign against the EU's position on water services liberalization. Even while operating on the margins of the political process, NGOs successfully improved the input legitimacy of EU trade politics by serving as educators and agenda setters, generating awareness, giving a voice to broader societal concerns at the EU, national and municipal levels. However, as in the access to medicines case and despite support from some EU member states, members of the European Parliament, and key players in the EU's water industry, the robust legal-liberal episteme hamstrung NGO efforts to bring about substantive and normative changes in external trade policy.

The first part of this chapter provides a brief account of the entrenchment of services in the international trade regime and the resulting expansion of the legal-liberal episteme. The remainder of the chapter then traces the role of NGOs in the development of the EU's position on water services liberalization in the context of GATS negotiations during the Doha Development Round. Due to the highly technical nature of trade in services negotiations, together with their complex bilateral, request-offer format, EU experts and technocrats working in DG Trade were empowered in the external trade policymaking process relative to other actors. They were able to insulate important decisions from public scrutiny and to effectively marginalize and de-legitimize NGOs by emphasizing flaws, hyperbole, or misunderstandings in their advocacy. In so doing, EU experts and technocrats successfully deflected criticism and exercised their distinct, functional authority to develop external trade policy on water services that "fit" within the legal-liberal episteme.

For a moment, NGOs and their supporters rejoiced as the EU tabled its bilateral requests and shifted its attention to negotiating GATS commitments through plurilateral, collective requests, which do not address water for human use. However, it remains evident more than 10 years later that the EU is committed to pursuing water services liberalization of this nature, particularly through GATS "Plus" provisions in free trade agreements, mega-regional agreements, EPAs, and, possibly, through the newly proposed plurilateral international TiSA. This chapter concludes that the EU has not undergone a substantive or normative shift in policy as a result of NGO pressure but simply shifted forums to deflect, silence, and marginalize the NGO-led campaign.

Locking services liberalization into the multilateral trade regime

The GATS contains the first set of multilateral rules governing the liberalization of international trade in services. The concept of "trade in services" originally appeared in a report on international competitiveness commissioned by the OECD. This group of econo-mists was the first to acknowledge the growing proportion of services-related cross-border transactions and to consider that conventional "trade concepts" such as protectionism could be applied to transac-tions in services.[4] In the face of the new protectionism of the late 1970s, the mantel of trade in services was taken up by US-based mul-tinational firms which launched a consciousness-raising campaign and international coalition-building exercise aimed at focusing the interna-tional trade liberalization agenda on services. Services were touted by US trade officials, industry analysts, academics, and corporate lobby-ists alike as a panacea for international competitiveness and further liberalization of the global economy.

By 1982, the United States' Coalition of Services Industries and the Liberalization of Trade in Services Committee in Britain were formed and, together with other business lobbies such as the International Chamber of Commerce, became staunch advocates of a new round of GATT negotiations that would place services on the agenda. For Drake and Nicolaides, "by the mid-1980s there was a large and still expanding multinational 'trade in services mafia'."[5] The United States aggressively pushed the services issue at the behest of its services lobby at the GATT ministerial meeting in Geneva in 1982. Fearing the power of the American services industry and reluctant to liberalize their own services industries, the Europeans advocated a "go slow approach." Developing countries were initially opposed to any inclusion of services in the GATT because they believed that such an agreement could undermine their ability to pursue national policy objectives and con-strain their regulatory powers.[6] Yet countries agreed to launch nego-tiations on services, "to establish a multilateral framework of principles and rules for trade in services with a view to expand such trade under conditions of transparency and progressive liberalization, and as a means of promoting the economic growth of all trading partners and the development of developing countries."[7]

Uruguay Round negotiations on services were fraught with periods of brinkmanship, controversy, and deep compromise, particularly with respect to the scope of the rules and the inclusion of the MFN princi-ple as a general obligation. These challenges notwithstanding, services negotiations were widely viewed as key to global economic growth. The EU, in particular, stood to gain the most from a concluded deal given that Western Europe accounted for almost half of world trade in services by the mid-1980s and European service-sector growth was expected to outpace that of the United States.[8] Moreover, and despite early reservations, some developing countries became proponents of the evolving services agreement and sought to shape it in their own interests. This shift is largely due to the growing presence and activism of private, non-state actors and the importance of services in developing economies particularly as they abandoned import-substitution programs and sought to implement market-oriented policies in line with International Monetary Fund (IMF) and World Bank obligations. In Sylvia Ostry's view, "many developing countries began to see reform of key service sectors such as telecommunications as essential building blocks in the soft infrastructure underpinning growth and the GATS as a means to furthering domestic reform."[9]

The GATS is a comprehensive legal framework of rules and disciplines that covers all internationally traded services[10] except those provided in the exercise of government authority "neither on a commercial basis, or in competition with one or more suppliers,"[11] and all services related to the exercise of traffic rights.[12] It also reflects the complex nature of international transactions in services by defining four ways or "modes" of supplying services: cross-border supply (Mode 1), consumption abroad (Mode 2), commercial presence (Mode 3), and temporary movement of natural persons (Mode 4).

Although the initiative to shift services into the multilateral trade regime originated in the United States, the EU/developing country preference for a "soft" framework agreement is reflected in the bottom-up or positive list approach to liberalization in the GATS. Specific market access and national treatment commitments are listed in "schedules" and are negotiated bilaterally in a request-offer format on a sector-by-sector basis. Commitments are then multilateralized according to the MFN principle. Members may also make "horizontal commitments"—market access and national treatment commitments that apply across all sectors and usually pertain to a particular mode of supply. However, WTO members are also free to schedule market access, national treatment, and horizontal limitations in negative lists. For example, a country may choose to open its market to foreign banks but may limit the total number of operators by specifying a market access limitation. A government may also restrict the number of service workers who may enter the country via Mode 4, regardless of the sector in which they plan to work.

Taken together, these flexibilities provide members a great deal of latitude to decide which sectors to liberalize and to what extent. However, scheduling positive and negative lists requires considerable foresight and expertise. Once commitments and limitations are scheduled they become legally "bound" or locked-in like tariffs under the GATT Agreement and actionable in WTO dispute settlement. It would be very costly to a country if it chose to renege on services liberalization commitments. This challenge would become the focal point of the NGO-led campaign against the GATS, and water services liberalization specifically.

The extent of liberalization commitments made during the Uruguay Round was quite modest.[13] Although 96 WTO members made commitments in services, Hoekman estimates that developed countries scheduled 45 percent of their service sectors while low and middle-income countries scheduled only 12 percent.[14] Extensive market access and national treatment limitations means that only a fraction of service commitments are without exceptions—25 percent in developed countries and 7 percent in developing countries—and are concentrated in Modes 1 (50 percent), 2 (30 percent) and 3 (20 percent).[15] Also, the majority of commitments had been taken in the least sensitive sectors such as tourism and business services rather than education or health. Across the board, the commitments did not present many new business opportunities but rather bound already existing market openings. The GATS (Article XIX) has a "built-in" mandate to further liberalize international trade in services; GATS negotiations began in January 2000 and, since 2001, have been part of the single undertaking under the DDA.

NGO backlash to the GATS: spotlight on water services liberalization

The launch of the DDA and a new round of GATS negotiations occurred alongside brewing concern over the implications of the GATS for national autonomy, democracy, and the ability of governments to regulate in the public interest, particularly in poor countries. Beginning in 2000, a high-profile, global campaign against the so-called "GAT-SAttack"[16] was launched by NGOs such as the World Development Movement (WDM), Third World Network, Council of Canadians, ATTAC, Friends of the Earth (FOE), World Economy, Ecology and Development (WEED), and the mobilization of several important networks such as Our World is Not For Sale (OWINFS), GATSwatch, and the Seattle to Brussels network.[17] These organizations sought to educate the public about the implications of the GATS for public services and to mobilize them to protest against services liberalization.[18] The main concern is that GATS will act as a regulatory straightjacket, despite the bottom-up scheduling of commitments and other flexibilities noted above.[19] NGOs cite formidable practical obstacles to scheduling market access, national treatment, and horizontal limitations. In particular, many developed countries and least-developed countries lack the capacity, technical know-how, and expertise to foresee a need for future policy flexibility in particular sectors or modes of supply, and there are few options available if a country wishes to add protections and roll back liberalization at a later date once a commitment is scheduled.[20]

NGOs campaigning against the GATS claim that the agreement threatens access to basic public services, including drinking water and basic sanitation services.[21] While most NGOs acknowledge that the GATS does not require WTO members to privatize their public services, they are concerned that GATS commitments entrench rights for corporate service providers and that the nature of the agreement will make it very difficult, if not impossible, for governments to reverse failed privatization projects. Moreover, for sectors included in a GATS schedule, a country must have the expertise to anticipate future challenges and exempt monopolies (e.g. postal services, water distribution) and exclusive service supplier arrangements (e.g. post-secondary education, health care services) or risk facing disputes. Critics claim that this places a disproportionate burden on poor countries. Services provided in the exercise of governmental authority, defined as "services provided neither on a commercial basis nor in competition with one or more service suppliers" such as social security and immigration services, are exempt from coverage under the GATS.[22] However, public services are often provided in partnership with private actors and/or with private funding. NGOs claim that the introduction of commercial elements into public service delivery opens a window for GATS coverage and hence pressure to liberalize.[23] Finally, there is concern that developing countries face considerable pressure in FTA negotiations and by other institutions such as the World Bank and IMF to privatize and liberalize public services.[24] In response to these challenges, NGOs and other members of civil society have called for public services to be carved-out or exempted from the GATS.[25]

Many consider the liberalization of water services, particularly for human use and basic sanitation, as tantamount to the commodification of life-giving resources. When it became known in 2002 that the EU was aggressively pursuing water services liberalization in developing and least-developed countries—many of which had recently experienced water privatization disasters—it became the focal point of the campaign against GATS in Europe.[26]

European-based multinational corporations dominate the global water market. Indeed, three of the top four global water companies have their headquarters in the EU: Veolia Environment, Suez Environment, and United Utilities. Thus, the EU has a clear offensive interest in improving market access for European services providers in the water services sub-sector. However, DG Trade officials have also defended the requests for water services liberalization as an effort to promote sustainable development and to universalize water services. Facilitating the operation of European-based water companies in developing and least-developed countries was considered key to meeting the Millennium Development Goal of halving the proportion of people without access to sustainable access to safe drinking water and basic sanitation.[27] DG Trade officials take the position that where governments have undertaken to involve the private sector—usually in public-private partnerships (PPPs)—in the water services sub-sector, foreign companies should be allowed to bid for contracts. This point is significant since "by the end of 2000, at least 93 countries had partially privatized water or wastewater services and more than 65 percent were developing countries."[28] For DG Trade officials, European-based water companies will operate more efficiently, invest in basic infrastructure, provide better quality water services, and drive down prices paid by consumers, thereby working to ensure more equitable access to water supplies and sanitation services.[29]

In the context of GATS negotiations, the objective of DG Trade officials is to pursue the gradual liberalization of global trade in services in order to achieve real and meaningful market access opportunities for European service providers for their exports. Moreover, "properly regulated" services liberalization is considered a win-win scenario for development and growth for developed and developing countries alike.[30] By contrast, NGOs that are mobilized against the GATS and water services liberalization reject this premise wholesale. A fundamental disagreement over basic economic principles underlines this adversarial and largely unconstructive relationship and accounts for why the NGOs working on the water services issue sit on the margins of the external trade political process in Europe.

Secrets, leaks, and the launch of a campaign

Despite the creation of a wide range of participatory mechanisms at the EU level, there was little public consultation on services liberalization in the early days of GATS negotiations in the DDA. The highly technical and complex nature of services negotiations provided DG Trade officials with justification for keeping the substantive details of negotiations from public scrutiny. This changed in 2002 when the Canadian Polaris Institute covertly obtained the EU's draft requests for third-country market access and made them available to a small number of anti-GATS NGOs, including the WDM and the Corporate Europe Observatory (CEO), for a global Internet exposé. With the intent to derail GATS negotiations and undermine "secret trade diplomacy," the Polaris Institute and the CEO published the 29 draft requests on their websites on 16 April 2002.[31] The full text of the 109 final requests was subsequently leaked on 24 February 2003.[32]

While the potential impact of GATS on water services was on the radar of some NGOs between 2000 and 2002,[33] it did not become a focal point for NGOs opposing GATS until after the EU requests were leaked. In response, the campaign adopted a multi-pronged strategy involving grassroots mobilization, public demonstrations and rallies, petitions, and reports on the potential negative impact of services liberalization on public services, environment, and democracy.[34] The belief that the GATS "is the wrong treaty, in the wrong place, at the wrong time"[35] underscored protests against services liberalization and came to define the campaign against the EU's requests for water services liberalization abroad.

International media erupted in a furor over the EU's requests for third-country market access.[36] It was widely reported that the EU was demanding that essential services be traded for concessions in other areas being negotiated during the DDA. For instance, after receiving copies of the 29 draft requests, the UK's *Guardian* newspaper reported that "[t]he European Union is demanding full-scale privatization of public monopolies across the world as its price for dismantling the Common Agricultural Policy in the new round of global trade talks."[37] Similarly, the requests only served to confirm the gravest fears of NGOs over the EU's so-called "hidden agenda" to dismantle the public sector in developing countries.[38] In the immediate aftermath of the leak, NGOs coined the requests a "privatizers' hit list"[39] and condemned the EU for "preparing to trample all over sustainable development objectives in the naked pursuit of the interests of European multinational service corporations."[40] Following the leak of the full text of the requests, WDM reported: "now we can see that the EU is aiming for a global takeover of essential services and the financial infrastructure of developing countries for the benefit of EU corporations."[41] Most egregious, according to the campaign, was the EU's requests for water services liberalization commitments from 72 WTO members including Bolivia and South Africa, two countries that had recently experienced water privatization disasters.[42] The requests were presented as evidence of the EU's agenda to dismantle public water delivery in developing and least-developed countries regardless of the devastating record of private-sector involvement in many of the targeted countries.

It was clear to DG Trade officials from this moment that neither compromise nor co-optation would be possible with NGOs working on this issue.[43] They tried to downplay the significance of the leak and, at the same time, began to cast their critics as outsiders by publicly de-legitimizing their work and concerns. They worked through the media to portray the NGO reaction as hyperbole and to counter fundamental "misunderstandings" being circulated about the nature and content of the GATS negotiations. In an official reaction, the European Commission issued a public statement that characterized the leak as "unfortunate" and "irresponsible"; the drafts, it said, are a work in progress and do not reflect the official EU position since consultations with EU member states were not yet complete.[44] Although the response to the requests had generated "wild accusations," the Commission hoped that critics would see that the draft requests did not ask any countries to privatize or deregulate their public and essential services. Any claim that the GATS negotiations undermine the provision of public services was characterized as "completely wrong."[45]

In a second move, DG Trade tried to keep the lid on boiling public reactions to the leaked text by responding to demands for greater transparency and public input into GATS negotiations. Over 90 organizations had issued an open letter calling for greater public disclosure of GATS requests and offers, a more integral consultative role for the EP, and a full moratorium on GATS negotiations at least until a "full evaluation and impact assessment of the consequences of the current or proposed GATS obligations" is undertaken in cooperation with civil society.[46] The EP echoed these demands in a March 2003 resolution.[47] DG Trade responded by opening up space in the CSD for discussion of the GATS negotiations but most NGOs active in the campaign saw the move as too little, too late and elected not to attend. Those that did attend were deeply critical of the question-answer format of meetings and the lack of rigorous debate.[48]

Fearing co-optation and seeing no possibility for compromise, NGOs turned their attention away from DG Trade to focus on developing an EU-wide public education campaign aimed at disseminating information about the dangers associated with water services liberalization and privatization. The objective was to raise awareness, stimulate public discussion and debate, and mobilize pressure against the inclusion of water services in the EU's requests for third-country market access. By 2002 there was very little direct contact between DG Trade and NGOs working on the GATS except in the form of protest letters, and the campaign operated almost entirely outside the formal political process discussed in Chapter 2.

Led by Oxfam, WDM, ATTAC, FOE International, Save the Children, and a Belgian umbrella organization of development NGOs, the Coalition of the Flemish North-South Movement 11.11.11, the campaign used major public demonstrations at the municipal, national, and EU levels as the primary means of mobilizing public awareness and support. For example, a "European Day of Action Against GATS" took place in several cities across Europe on 13 March 2003.[49] In addition to the countless protest letters sent directly to Commission officials calling for the removal of water from the EU's GATS requests, NGOs also used a range of high-profile meetings to stage protests against the EU and the commercialization of water services more generally. For example, at the Third World Water Forum in Kyoto, Japan, NGOs made a plea to the ministerial conference to "keep water and water services out of the WTO and all other regional and international trade and investment negotiations and agreements."[50] NGOs took the opportunity to present position papers and to speak widely about the risks associated with water liberalization and privatization.[51] NGOs also launched an "Evian Challenge" in advance of the G8 summit in Evian, France in 2003, calling on EU member states such as Germany and France to withdraw the EU's water requests.[52]

Another key feature of the campaign was the dissemination of information through press releases, briefings, and information booklets. A number of NGOs such as Save the Children and Oxfam International produced comprehensive analyses of the risks associated with making water liberalization commitments under GATS.[53] Others highlighted the negative experiences of water privatization in developing countries.[54] Organizations such as WDM sought to educate national parliamentarians and members of the EP directly through a series of briefings.

There was also a distinct grassroots dimension to the campaign. NGOs campaigned in municipalities and lobbied local officials and national members of parliament in an effort to get them to exert pressure on their national representatives to remove water from the EU's GATS requests. The Coalition of the North-South Movement 11.11.11, ATTAC, and WDM were especially active in this respect, orchestrating postcard and letter campaigns, demonstrations, and sit-ins whereby national and municipal governments were flooded with demands for support. In a sign of solidarity with the campaign, hundreds of municipalities across Europe declared themselves "GATS-free zones" and passed municipal motions in opposition to the GATS negotiations.[55] The Assembly of European Regions, which represents 250 member regions from 33 European countries and 14 interregional organizations, also declared that it strongly opposed any liberalization in the cultural, education, health, social affairs, water supply, and purification services sectors, especially in the context of GATS negotiations.[56] These symbolic moves highlight substantial local resistance to the EU's agenda in GATS negotiations and solidarity with the campaign more generally.

The campaign also resonanced with national members of parliament across the EU. For instance, during the first session of the Scottish Parliament in 2003, 70 parliamentarians signed motions calling for more parliamentary and public debate on services liberalization in the context of the GATS negotiations. German parliamentarians went several steps farther in the summer of 2003, when the Bundestag asked the German government to demand that the EU withdraw its external requests for water services liberalization.[57] Belgian parliamentarians made a similar call in December 2002 and again in April 2005. Although Belgium went unsupported by other EU member states, these moves represent major successes for the NGO-led campaign in the national context.[58]

It is also evident that the campaign resonated with European-based water companies. While they were instrumental in drafting the initial requests (2000–02),[59] they publicly and explicitly backed away from supporting the EU's position on water services liberalization following the leaked draft requests. According to Pascal Kerneis, managing director of the ESF, water companies got cold feet after the initial bad press from NGOs and no longer wanted to be publicly associated with any link between GATS and water services delivery in developing countries. Instead, they preferred to quietly pursue PPPs in developing countries.[60] In a series of statements, Thames, Suez, and Vivendi (now Veolia) used the World Water Forum in 2003 to publicly dissociate themselves from the GATS. Thames Water has been especially vocal about its opposition to the EU's water requests and has explicitly asked the Commission not to "include water or waste water services in its demands for the forthcoming GATS round" as the company "both will respect and share the concerns raised by civil society organizations."[61] At a symposium organized by the Institute for Public Policy Research and sponsored by Thames Water in Brussels, "[a]ll the European water companies present denied they had asked the EU Commission to insert water into the 72 requests."[62]

Clearly the campaign against the GATS and water services liberalization improved the input legitimacy of EU trade politics during this period. NGOs were instrumental in educating the public and parliamentarians about the issue, they gave voice to broader, developing country concerns, and they successfully generated EU-wide awareness and debate about a largely unknown policy issue. The campaign also compelled EU-based water companies to take a stand with members of civil society against the EU. This occurred despite their offensive, market access interests and the fact that NGOs worked from outside the EU's formal political process. These improvements in democratic process notwithstanding, a closer look at the development of external trade policy beyond 2002 suggests that the campaign did not bring about substantive or normative policy change. Rather, DG Trade officials held fast to the idea that water services liberalization in developing countries is essential to meeting sustainable development priorities and universalizing access to clean drinking water and sanitation. Criticisms of water services liberalization were largely incomprehensible to DG Trade officials because they were at odds with the dominant political agenda, intersubjective ideas, and ideological beliefs that framed external trade policymaking at the time. Instead, DG Trade officials tweaked at the margins of their GATS requests for third-country market access in the hopes of silencing critics while continuing to pursue water services liberalization in developing countries.[63]

Request, react, rejoice?

Progress in the DDA began to languish after the 2003 WTO Ministerial Conference in Cancun collapsed as the result of an overcrowded agenda and deep divisions over crucial issues such as agriculture.[64] In the following months, services negotiations showed no signs of progress. Despite the original deadline of 31 March 2003,[65] only 42 services offers covering 57 WTO members (the EU offer covered 15 members) had been submitted by April 2004. The "July Package" served to revitalize the DDA in mid-2004. Annex C pertained to services and called on members to ensure "a high quality of offers, particularly in sectors and modes of supply of export interest to developing countries, with special attention to be given to least-developed countries."[66] The new deadline for approved services offers was set for 31 May 2005.

Where the EU's defensive interests (services offers) were concerned, DG Trade held several consultations with civil society. In addition to three CSD meetings prior to Cancun, DG Trade launched an unprecedented request for public input into how the EU should respond in its initial offer to the requests for market access it had received from third countries. Thousands of responses to the consultation document were received prior to the release of the EU's services offer in April 2003.

Where the EU's offensive interests (services requests) were concerned, it was a different story. DG Trade officials pulled farther and farther away from the participatory political process following the leak of the EU's requests as they worked to insulate the offensive agenda from public scrutiny and reinvigorate GATS negotiations. No CSD meetings on services took place between the collapse of talks at Cancun in September 2003 and the July Package in 2004. When the CSD sessions on services resumed on 9 December 2004, participants were informed of the Commission's intent to revise the third-country market access requests. NGOs were reportedly shocked by this announcement since revisions were not required by the WTO and there was no public announcement of a revision of the EU requests in advance of this meeting, nor an invitation for consultation as there was for the services offers.[67] Senior-level DG Trade officials explained the political rationale behind the revisions but were vague on the substance of the requests. Dialogue during this CSD meeting was instead limited to a heated exchange between DG Trade officials and NGOs over whether services negotiations are about pushing privatization. In response to demands for greater transparency, the revisions were defended as a closed-door matter.[68] The next CSD services meeting would not take place again until 13 May 2005, long after the revised requests had been submitted to the WTO, the last opportunity for public dialogue between DG Trade officials and civil society before the Hong Kong Ministerial Meeting in December 2005.

At first glance, it appears as though the campaign against water services liberalization had some impact because the EU's revised requests struck a decidedly more "development-friendly" tone and removed some of the language NGOs found most offensive.[69] Where water services are concerned, two changes are significant. First, to better take into account the level of development of individual WTO members, the EU reduced the number of requests directed at LDCs from three out of five to two out of five sectors, which include telecommunications, financial services, transport, construction, and environmental services—key "sectors in which the [EU] can offer extensive expertise and technological skills whilst at the same time representing its export interests."[70] Nevertheless, water services remained squarely on the table in the EU's revised requests, even for the world's poorest countries. Since LDCs are generally thought to be exempt from taking commitment in the current round of GATS negotiations, NGOs consider the two out of five benchmarking strategy to be unnecessarily aggressive and evidence of the EU's continued quest to "prise open fragile financial and public utilities markets in some of the world's poorest nations."[71]

Second, while the EU's requests cover all environmental sub-sectors including water for human use, the revisions aimed to clarify and limit their scope. In the initial requests, the EU had asked for open-ended market access. The revisions make clear that for modes 1 (cross-border trade) and 2 (consumption abroad), the EU is requesting national treatment and market access commitments primarily for advisory or consulting services. Where "other" environmental services are mentioned, the EU is only requesting market access and national treatment for environmental impact assessment and environmental risk analysis, two key activities for sustainable development. Most relevant for the anti-GATS campaign are the EU's requests for Mode 3 (commercial presence). Where infrastructure services (water and solid/hazardous waste) are concerned, the revised requests draw a distinction "between services supplied directly to business, where more ambitious commitments are sought, and the traditional public services (notably municipal services), where the request is more focused."[72] For services that are subject to exclusive or monopoly rights the EU asks that foreign companies not be discriminated against in the allocation of concessions or in the operation of a service, if granted a tender. Finally, for services that are not subject to exclusive or monopoly rights, the EU continues to request that countries take full market access and national treatment commitments. According to Peter Mandelson (trade commissioner 2004–08), the revised requests "simply aim to facilitate the opening up of these services to international operators if and when the responsible public authorities freely choose to do so, for instance through any form of public-private partnership of their choice."[73] In essence, this is the same request made in 2002 but it is now couched in explicit assurances that the EU does not actively seek to dismantle public delivery of essential services or undermine exclusive service provider arrangements, at least when they are included in GATS services schedules.

DG Trade officials sought to make the revised requests more politically palatable to developing countries and to correct the messages being conveyed by NGOs about the EU's hidden offensive interests.[74] They were keen to convince the public and parliamentarians alike that NGO concerns about GATS and water privatization are baseless. Indeed, senior-level DG Trade officials described NGO criticisms as "nonsensical," "emotionally charged," "without merit," "not grounded in reality," and "fundamentally flawed" during several interviews.[75] The WTO struck a similar tone in its information pamphlet entitled, "Misunderstandings and Scare Stories: The WTO is not after your water."[76] These reactions indicate that the campaign had some effect by making DG Trade officials more sensitive to wider public concerns.

They adjusted their language and tempered their offensive approach accordingly but they did not change the substance of the requests in any significant way to meet the demands of NGOs.

Prior to the 2005 Hong Kong Ministerial Conference, few countries had responded to the EU's revised requests. Indeed, only 71 countries submitted initial offers and only 32 countries submitted revised offers.[77] In order to push forward services negotiations, WTO members agreed in Hong Kong to pursue plurilateral negotiations alongside bilateral negotiations. While participation in the plurilateral negotiations is voluntary, members were urged to consider collective requests and "to participate actively in these negotiations towards achieving a progressively higher level of liberalization of trade in services, with appropriate flexibility for individual developing countries as provided for in Article XIX of the GATS."[78] The EU chaired the Friends of Environmental Services Group and, in February 2006, presented 22 targeted countries with collective market access requests for environmental services.[79] Notably, the collective requests explicitly exclude water for human use but include water services for other purposes such as sanitation and sewage.[80]

Some consider this exclusion to be a sign that the EU has backed away from its requests for water services liberalization.[81] This conclusion is both premature and short sighted. The politically contentious nature of the plurilateral request-offer process itself and the fact that partners in the plurilateral process do not share the same strategic interests in this sector help explain why water for human use was left off the table in these negotiations. Moreover, Norway, a member of the Friends of Environmental Services Group, formally withdrew its requests in a range of sensitive essential service sectors including energy, higher education, and water in December 2005. It would have been politically impossible for Norway to participate in the collective requests had water for human use been part of the demands. Moreover, both the EU and United States made it clear at the Hong Kong ministerial that plurilateral and bilateral negotiations are complementary, not mutually exclusive, tracts.

Despite the EU's best efforts to push forward GATS negotiations, they have largely been at a standstill for the better part of a decade. Momentum for the collective requests died when the DDA negotiations were suspended in 2006 and then collapsed again in 2008. The limited success of the Bali Ministerial has not worked to kick-start GATS negotiations. This situation is owing to the loss of momentum in the DDA more generally, rather than to a lack of ambition with respect to water services liberalization or a change of position within the EU. Indeed, EU bilateral requests are best described as "tabled" or on hold while it pursues its services-related commercial interests outside the DDA.

The EU is currently negotiating a plurilateral Trade in Services Agreement (TiSA) alongside 23 other WTO members with the aim of reaching an ambitious agreement that includes all trade in services covered by the GATS. Although the negotiations formally take place outside the WTO, the hope is that the agreement will serve as a gold standard for services liberalization, generate a critical mass of support among WTO members, and become multilateralized in the future. Widely criticized for its secrecy, little is known about the content of the TiSA agreement. Draft TiSA texts leaked by WikiLeaks have sparked widespread condemnation but reveal only a little about the extent to which environmental services, and water services in particular, will be included.[82] Based on the only leaked market access request documents available—for Turkey and Israel—it is clear that the EU is seeking commitments in several water sub-sectors including sewage, refuse disposal, and sanitation and similar services, even though the EU has stated it will not, itself, take any commitments in TiSA on water collection, purification, distribution, and management services. It is precisely this sort of EU double standard that catalyzed NGOs in the anti-GATS campaign.

There is also concern that the TiSA includes GATS "Plus" provisions that bind members to more stringent disciplines than are required by the GATS. Chief among these are the "standstill" and "ratchet" provisions which respectively "lock-in" current levels of liberalization across the board and preclude a return to public models once the decision to privatize a sector is taken.[83] Given that many of the same countries are parties to two or more of the agreements, the TiSA will likely provide the backbone for services liberalization in the ongoing negotiation of mega-regionals such as the Comprehensive Economic Trade Agreement (CETA), the Transatlantic Trade and Investment Partnership (TTIP), and the Transpacific Partnership (TPP). The inclusion of investor-to-state dispute settlement (ISDS) in the mega-regionals—a mechanism that allows investors to sue governments for perceived violations of their investor rights—would make the scheduling and enforcement of liberalization commitments (including those for water services) even more robust in the mega-regionals than the GATS which is supported by the WTO's state-to-state dispute settlement system. It would also likely lead to what De Ville and Siles-Brügge refer to as "regulatory chill"—a situation where governments fear the costs of arbitration disputes and are thus reluctant to regulate in the public interest and/or roll back privatization and liberalization commitments as they deem fit.[84]

It is too soon to assess the extent to which water services liberalization will be locked in through the negotiation of these new agreements. However, when considered in light of the EU's *Global Europe*[85] strategy and related bilateral agreements and negotiations, it is clear that water services liberalization continues to be viewed as a win-win process addressing the EU's major offensive commercial interests and promoting development in poor countries.[86] For example, many of the EU's developing, bilateral trade partners have taken a vast range of commitments to liberalize water services with few exemptions in the areas of sewage, wastewater, and sanitation.[87] No country has yet taken a commitment to liberalize the distribution of drinking water but giving market access to European-based water companies in some subsectors potentially opens the door for future expansion into water for human use. Moreover, the EU has several bilateral negotiations underway that may cover drinking water distribution by inclusion in the proposed agreements' investment chapters, as is the case with the stalled Mercado Común del Sur (MERCOSUR) negotiations[88] and the ongoing CETA negotiations.[89] The EU has also begun to negotiate bilateral services agreements using a negative list—as opposed to a GATS-style positive list—approach, whereby market access and national treatment generally apply to all services sectors except where specific exclusions are listed in the annexes to the agreement. This would require the liberalization of non-exempt services when and if the government decided to privatize a public-sector service, such as water distribution.[90] This is the approach being taken in the EU-Ukraine Deep and Comprehensive Free Trade Area (DCFTA), which will also likely serve as a model for future bilateral negotiations with developing countries.[91]

In addition, the EU actively promotes the involvement of European-based water companies in developing countries through parallel aid initiatives and the political and financial support of public-private partnerships in the water sector. For example, the ACP-EU Water Facility is funded by the European Development Fund and was created to improve access to clean drinking water and basic sanitation in ACP countries by supporting investment in PPPs, in which EU-based water companies are major players. The EU also funds wider initiatives aimed at improving the business climate for PPPs such as the ACP Business Climate (BizClim).[92] Several individual EU member states are major donors, alongside the European Bank for Reconstruction and Development, for the Public-Private Infrastructure Advisory Facility (PPIAF), an initiative that aims "to help eliminate poverty and achieve sustainable development through public-private partnerships in infrastructure," but which in practice actively supports privatization in a range of sectors including water and sanitation in developing countries.[93] Beyond aid, the European Investment Bank—the EU's public bank which actively promotes EU policy through its lending practices— has been widely criticized by NGOs for pushing water privatization projects in developing countries.[94] While this is not an exhaustive examination, these examples show that the EU continues to develop and pursue trade and development policy based on the normative understanding that water services liberalization and the involvement of the private sector in the delivery of these services is a win for development, despite the oppositional and public education campaigns waged by NGOs in Europe.

In the meantime, NGOs abandoned the campaign against water services liberalization and the GATS by late 2005. The stalling of the DDA and effective forum shifting by the Commission deflected criticism and NGO priorities shifted to new issues such as anti-austerity in the wake of the global financial crisis, inclusion of ISDS in mega-regional agreements, and to sustainable development and poverty alleviation more generally. No new actors have mobilized in their place and the EU's continued pursuit of water services liberalization abroad and opportunities for PPPs in water services delivery in developing countries goes largely unchecked today.[95]

Conclusion

This chapter told two stories. One story is of an NGO-led protest campaign that succeeded in educating the public and parliamentarians alike about an arcane trade agreement. By framing the GATS and water services liberalization issues in terms of human rights and democracy, NGOs were able to mobilize widespread support and action at the municipal, national, and EU levels and give voice to those who would be impacted by the proposed trade deals. They improved the transparency of policymaking by effectively using access to information requests to peel back the curtain on the relationship between EU experts and technocrats working in DG Trade and EU-based water companies. Leaking the details of draft negotiating texts further exposed EU policymakers to scrutiny. By publicizing their grievances in the media, NGOs demanded that EU policymakers answer difficult questions and defend their actions and policies, thereby improving their accountability. These achievements unquestionably improved the input legitimacy of the external trade policymaking process in Europe.

Yet, most of this took place in the streets and in the media, far away from the formal political process established at the EU level.

The second story is one of a tempest in a teapot. Despite all of the successes of the campaign against water services liberalization, NGOs were unable to bring about substantive policy change. This was owing to fundamental, normative disagreements over the purpose and potential consequences of water services liberalization. EU technocrats and experts are developing policy from within the legal-liberal episteme. They are guided by the belief that water services liberalization can be a win-win process, serving both the EU's major offensive commercial interests and serving development priorities in poor countries. Indeed, water services liberalization is seen as essential to securing universal access to safe drinking water and basic sanitation. By contrast, water services liberalization was widely panned by the NGO-led campaign as serving the interests of EU-based corporations, undermining the rights of the world's most vulnerable people to basic necessities, and constituting a massive attack on the ability of governments to regulate in the public interest. These arguments were, and still are, unintelligible to EU trade experts and technocrats, regardless of how well supported they were by the public, parliamentarians, and even some major water companies. Given the intractability of these two positions, EU policymakers adopted a two-fold strategy to deflect the NGO-led campaign. They de-legitimized NGOs by highlighting their lack of knowledge and understanding of technical trade issues, and they pulled away from the political process to develop policy behind closed doors. They were empowered to do so by virtue of the highly technical and secretive nature of services negotiations. Functional authority pooled in the hands of EU experts and technocrats and it remains in place there today. Water services liberalization is well underway and the inclusion of water for human use is still very much "on the table" in the EU's mega-regional and bilateral trade negotiations. The strength of the legal-liberal episteme insulated EU experts and technocrats to pursue water services liberalization and to seek out market opportunities for EU-based water companies despite very effective NGO campaigning and public mobilization around the issue.

Notes

1 In the GATS, water-related sub-sectors are negotiated under environmental services. In the EU's requests, water for human use includes water collection, purification, and distribution. Also included in the sub-sector are sewage services, refuse disposal services, sanitation, and similar services.

2 Maude Barlow, *Blue Future: Protecting Water for People and the Planet Forever* (Toronto, Canada: House of Anansi Press, 2013).

3 Michael Strange, "Why Network Across National Borders? TANs, their Discursivity, and the Case of the Anti-GATS Campaign," *Journal of Civil Society* 7, no. 1 (2011): 63–79.

4 William J. Drake and Kalypso Nicolaides, "Ideas, Interests, and Institutionalization: Trade in Services and the Uruguay Round," *International Organization* 46, no. 1 (1992): 45–46.

5 Drake and Nicolaides, "Ideas, Interests, and Institutionalization," 60.

6 J.P. Singh, "The Evolution of National Interests: New Issues and North-South Negotiations During the Uruguay Round," in *Negotiating Trade: Developing Countries in the WTO and NAFTA*, ed. John S. Odell (Cambridge: Cambridge University Press, 2006), 61–63; Gilbert R. Winham, "The Prenegotiation Phase of the Uruguay Round," *International Journal* 44 (1989): 280–303; and Fred Lazar, "Services and the GATT: US Motives and a Blueprint for Negotiations," *Journal of World Trade* 24, no. 1 (1990): 135–145.

7 Punta del Este Declaration Part II, www.sice.oas.org/trade/Punta_e.asp.

8 Gilbert Winham, "An Interpretive History of the Uruguay Round Negotiation," in *The World Trade Organization: Legal, Economic, and Political Analysis*, ed. Patrick Macrory, Arthur Appelton, and Michael Plummer (New York: Springer, 2005), 12.

9 Sylvia Ostry, "The Uruguay Round North-South Grand Bargain: Implications for Future Negotiations," *Political Economy of International Trade Law* (2000): 285–300.

10 Services sectors include: business services; communication services including postal services, courier services, telecommunication services, audiovisual services; construction and related engineering services; distribution services including postal and courier services; educational services; environmental services including sewage services, refuge disposal services, sanitation and similar services; financial services; health related and social services; tourism and travel related services; recreational, cultural and sporting services; transport services; and "other."

11 GATS Article 1c.

12 GATS Annex on Air Transport Services. Although a services sectoral classification list (WTO, "Services Sectoral Classification List," Note by the Secretariat, MTN.GNS/W/120, 10 July 1991) was compiled, no services except those mentioned are excluded *a priori* from negotiations.

13 Laura Altinger and Alice Enders, "The Scope and Depth of GATS Commitments," *The World Economy* 19, no. 3 (1996): 307–332.

14 Hoekman quoted in Rupa Chandra, "GATS and its Implications for Developing Countries: Key Issues and Concerns," DESA Discussion Paper 25, *United Nations Department of Economic and Social Affairs* (New York: United Nations, 2002), 7–8.

15 Chandra, "GATS and its Implications for Developing Countries," 8.

16 So-called for the first major petition against the GATS, "Stop the GATS Attack!" See Public Citizen, "Stop the GATS Attack!," 17 July 2002, www. citizen.org/trade/article_redirect.cfm?ID=1584.

17 See Michael Strange, *Writing Global Trade Governance: Discourse and the WTO* (Abingdon: Routledge, 2013); and Amandine Cresby, "A Dialogue

of the Deaf? Conflicting Discourses Over the EU," *The British Journal of Politics and International Relations* 16, no. 1 (2014): 168–187.

18 Public Citizen, "Stop the GATS Attack!"

19 See Scott Sinclair and Grieshaber-Otto, *Facing the Facts: A Guide to the GATS Debate* (Ottawa: Canadian Center for Policy Alternatives, 2002).

20 Rudolph Adlung, "Public Services in the GATS," *Journal of International Economic Law* 9, no. 2 (2006): 455–485; and Markus Krajewski, "Public Services and Trade Liberalization: Mapping the Legal Framework," *Journal of International Economic Law* 6, no. 2 (2003): 341–367.

21 Lyla Mehta and Birgit La Cour Madsen, "Is the WTO After Your Water? The General Agreement on Trade in Services (GATS) and Poor People's Right to Water," *Natural Resources Forum* 29 (2005): 154–164, 161.

22 GATS Article I(3)(b) and (c).

23 Maude Barlow, "The Last Frontier," *The Ecologist*, February 2001, www.ratical.org/co-globalize/lastfront.html.

24 Public Citizen, "Stop the GATS Attack."

25 As of 17 July 2002, 543 organizations had signed up to the "Stop the GATS Attack" statement.

26 In 2002, the EU included water and sanitation services in 72 of 109 third-country market access requests, 14 of which are directed at opening markets in least-developed countries.

27 For example, this position was conveyed by Commission officials during a question and answer period with the European Parliament on 5 October 2005, www.europarl.europa.eu/sides/getDoc.do?type=QT&reference=H-20 04-0327&language=BG.

28 Mehta and La Cour Madsen, "Is the WTO After Your Water?," 156.

29 Interview with Senior Trade Official, DG Trade, G1—Trade in Services and Investment; GATS and Investment, 14 June 2005.

30 According to the European Commission, "Summary of the EC's Revised Requests to Third Countries in the Services Negotiations under the DDA" (Brussels, 24 January 2005), "[t]hese requests DO seek to reduce restrictions and expand market access opportunities for European services companies and thus through increased competition bring lower prices and more choice to consumers and business in third country markets with a resulting increase in efficiency across the whole economy."

31 GATSwatch, "Leaked Confidential EU Documents Confirm Controversial Character of GATS Negotiations," *GATSwatch News*, 16 April 2002, www.gatswatch.org/leakannounce.html.

32 GATSwatch, "Initial GATS Offers," 10 April 2003, www.gatswatch.org/requests-offers.html#outgoing.

33 See for example FOE, "Stealing our Water: Implications of GATS for Global Water Resources," *FOE Briefing*, 2001; and John Hilary, *The Wrong Model: GATS, Trade Liberalization and Children's Right to Health* (London: Save the Children UK, 2001).

34 Jessica Woodroffe, "GATS: A Disservice to the Poor; The High Costs and Limited Benefits for Developing Countries of the General Agreement on Trade and Services," *World Development Movement*, 2002, www.iatp.org/files/GATS_A_Disservice_to_the_Poor.pdf.

35 FOE, "Stealing our Water."

36 For a sense of the media coverage following the leak of 29 draft requests and the leak of 109 final requests respectively, see www.gatswatch.org/ECleaknews.html and www.gatswatch.org/offreq-news.html.

37 John Vidal, Charlotte Denny, and Larry Elliot, "Secret Documents Reveal EU's Tough Stance on Global Trade," *The Guardian*, 17 April 2002.

38 See for instance World Development Movement's initial reaction at www.wdm.org.uk/news/archive/2002/EUleaks.htm.

39 Katherine Ainger, "A Privatisers' Hit List: European Commission Demands to Deregulate Services Spell Disaster for the Developing World," Comment, *The Guardian*, 18 April 2002.

40 GATSwatch, "GATS 2000 Negotiations—Reactions to Leaked EC Documents," www.gatswatch.org/ECleaknews.html.

41 WDM quoted in "Anti-GATS Campaigners Attack DTI," *The Guardian*, 25 February 2003, www.theguardian.com/politics/2003/feb/25/foreignpolicy.uk3.

42 Karen Bakker, *Privatizing Water: Governance Failure and the World's Urban Water Crisis* (Ithaca, NY: Cornell University Press).

43 Interview with Senior Trade Official, DG Trade, G1—Trade in Services and Investment; GATS and Investment, 14 June 2005.

44 Full text of the European Commission's official reaction is available at www.gatswatch.org/ECleaknews.html.

45 See www.gatswatch.org/ECleaknews.html .

46 The Open Letter to Commissioner Lamy and EU member states is available at www.gatswatch.org/070502letter-en.html.

47 European Parliament, "European Parliament Resolution on the General Agreement on Trade in Services (GATS) within the WTO, including Cultural Diversity," text adopted by the European Parliament (P5_TA[2003] 0087), 13 March 2003.

48 Interview with Marc Maes, European Policy Officer, Coalition of the Flemish North South Movement 11.11.11, Brussels, Belgium, 6 June 2005.

49 For an account of the protests in London, see FOE, "Archived Press Release: Spivs Sell Off Public Services through the WTO," 13 March 2003, www.foe.co.uk/resource/press_releases/spivs_sell_off_public_serv0.html.

50 The open letter is available at "A Civil Society Call to the Ministerial Conference at the Third World Water Forum, Kyoto, Japan, Keep Water and Water Services Out of the WTO," *IATP*, 1 May 2003, www.iatp.org/files/KEEP_WATER_AND_WATER_SERVICES_OUT_OF_THE_WTO.pdf.

51 See, for instance, the presentation by Maude Barlow, chairperson of the Council of Canadians, outlining NGO concerns regarding water services privatization: www.youtube.com/watch?v=pCEgQRmfqUE.

52 The Open Letter to members of the G8 is available at www.tni.org/article/evian-challenge-civil-society-call-eu-withdraw-its-gats-water-requests.

53 See, for instance, John Hilary, "GATS and WATER: The Threat of Services Negotiations at the WTO," A Save the Children briefing paper, 2003; Kevin Watkins, "International Trade Rules as an Obstacle to Development," in *Rigged Rules and Double Standards: Trade, Globalization and the Fight Against Poverty*, ed. Kevin Watkins and Penny Fowler (Oxford: Oxfam, 2002); and Claire Joy and Peter Hardstaff, *Whose Development Agenda? An Analysis of the European Union's GATS Requests of Developing Countries* (London: World Development Movement, 2003).

54 Public Citizen, "Water Privatization Fiascos: Broken Promises and Social Turmoil," A Special Report by Public Citizen's Water for All Program, 2003; Belanya et al., *Reclaiming Public Water: Achievements, Struggles, and Visions from Around the World* (Amsterdam: Transnational Institute [TNI]/Corporate Europe Observatory, 2005).

55 Michael Strange, *Writing Global Trade Governance: Discourse and the WTO* (Abingdon: Routledge, 2013), 156.

56 The Assembly of European Regions (AER), "Final Declaration—Reinforcing the Scope for Action by the Regions," Annual General Assembly, Vienna, 25–26 November 2004.

57 German Bundestag, "Securing Fair and Sustainable Trade Through a Comprehensive Development-Oriented World Trade Round," Motion … of the parliamentary fraction of the SPD in conjunction with … the parliamentary fraction of the BÜNDNIS 90/DIE GRÜNEN (Published Record 15/1317), 15th Legislative Session Status, 1 July 2003.

58 Christina Deckwirth, *The EU Corporate Trade Agenda: The Role and the Interests of Corporations and their Lobby Groups in Trade Policy-Making in the European Union* (Brussels and Berlin: Seattle 2 Brussels Network, 2005), www2.weed-online.org/uploads/s2b_eu_corporate_trade_agenda.pdf; and interview with Marc Maes, European Policy Officer, Coalition of the Flemish North South Movement 11.11.11, Brussels, Belgium, 6 June 2005.

59 The CEO obtained a large volume of email correspondence through access to documents requests that showed EU officials consulted extensively with European-based water companies prior to the drafting of the requests. They circulated a questionnaire on barriers to market access, held several seminars and private meetings.

60 Interview with Pascal Kerneis, Managing Director of the European Services Forum, 15 June 2005.

61 Letter from Richard Aylard, Head of Corporate Development and External Affairs RWE Thames Water to Francois-Charles Le Prevote, European Commission, DG Trade, 28 February 2005, quoted in Christina Deckwirth, "Water Almost Out of GATS?," *A Corporate Europe Observatory Briefing*, 2006.

62 Deckwirth, "Water Almost Out of GATS?"

63 Interview with Senior Trade Official, DG Trade, G1—Trade in Services and Investment; GATS and Investment, 14 June 2005.

64 Amrita Narlikar and Rorden Wilkinson, "Collapse at the WTO: A Cancun Post-Mortem," *Third World Quarterly* 25, no. 3 (2004): 447–460.

65 Only 15 WTO members had submitted offers by this deadline.

66 WTO, "Doha Work Programme," Decision adopted by the General Council (WT/L/579), 1 August 2004.

67 Interview with European Policy Officer, Coalition of the Flemish North-South Movement, 6 June 2005.

68 A summary report of the CSD meeting on 9 December, 2004 is available at trade.ec.europa.eu/doclib/cfm/doclib_section.cfm?sec=174&link_types= &diss=20&sta=561&en=580&page=29&langId=EN.

69 The following sentences were removed from the revised requests: 1 "Nevertheless, a number of barriers and obstacles to trade in environmental services remain, and the main objective of the [EU] for the negotiations is to reduce the barriers which European operators face in third countries'

markets"; 2 "The [EU] is seeking the removal of discrimination of, and restrictions to, European companies wishing to supply environmental services."

70 European Commission, "Summary of the EC's Revised Requests to Third Countries in the Services Negotiations under the DDA," 11.

71 Christian Aid, "GATS and the European Commission," *A Christian Aid Briefing Paper*, December 2005.

72 European Commission, "Summary of the EC's Revised Requests to Third Countries in the Services Negotiations under the DDA," 9.

73 Quoted in Deckwirth, "Water Almost Out of GATS?," 8.

74 Interview with Senior Trade Policy Official, DG Trade, G1—Trade in Services and Investment; GATS and Investment, 14 June 2005.

75 In addition to the interviews conducted by the author, an internal email exchange between a desk officer in DG Trade and Director-General Peter Carl obtained through an access to documents request reveals that DG Trade officials considered the campaign to be both seriously flawed and a serious threat to ongoing GATS negotiations. Deckwirth, "Water Almost Out of GATS?," 5.

76 WTO, "Misunderstandings and Scare Stories: The WTO is Not After Your Water," www.wto.org/english/tratop_e/serv_e/gats_factfiction8_e.htm.

77 For the list of countries, see European Services Forum, "GATS Initial Offers," www.esf.be/new/wto-negotiations/doha-development-agenda/offers/; and "GATS Revised Offers," www.esf.be/new/wto-negotiations/doha-devel opment-agenda/revised-offers/.

78 See World Trade Organization, "Ministerial Declaration, Adopted on 18 December 2005," Hong Kong (WT/MIN(05)/DEC), Item 26, www.wto. org/english/thewto_e/minist_e/min05_e/final_text_e.htm.

79 This group includes Australia, Canada, EU, Japan, Korea, Norway, Switzerland, the Separate Customs Territory of Taiwan, Penghu, Kinmen and Matsu, and the United States.

80 The text of the collective requests for environmental services is available from the ESF at www.esf.be/pdfs/Collective%20Requests/Environmental% 20Services%20C%20R.doc.

81 ICTSD, "Latin American Countries Band Together Against Water Liberalization," *Bridges Weekly Trade News Digest* 6, no. 6 (3 April 2006).

82 The latest leaks in June 2015 concern financial services, telecommunications, e-commerce, transportation, delivery services, movement of persons, and transparency. The leaked draft texts are available at wikileaks.org/tisa/.

83 Scott Sinclair and Hadrian Mertins-Kirkwood, "TISA versus Public Services," Public Services International Special Report: The Trade in Services Agreement and the Corporate Agenda, *Public Services International*, 28 April 2014, www.world-psi.org/sites/default/files/en_tisa_versus_public_ser vices_final_web.pdf.

84 Ferdi De Ville and Gabriel Siles-Brügge, *TTIP: The Truth about the Transatlantic Trade and Investment Partnership* (Bristol: Polity Press, 2015).

85 European Commission, "Global Europe: Competing the World," October 2006, trade.ec.europa.eu/doclib/docs/2006/october/tradoc_130376.pdf.

86 See Gabriel Siles-Brügge, *Constructing European Union Trade Policy: A Global Idea of Europe* (London: Palgrave Macmillan, 2014). A full list of EU bilateral agreements and negotiations is available by the European

Commission, "The EU's Bilateral Trade and Investment Agreements—Where are we?," Brussels, 1 August 2013, europa.eu/rapid/press-release_MEMO-13-734_en.htm.

87 See for example the 2012 EU-Central America Association Agreement tra de.ec.europa.eu/doclib/docs/2011/march/tradoc_147688.pdf, and the 2012 EU-Colombia and Peru FTA trade.ec.europa.eu/doclib/docs/2011/march/tradoc_147718.pdf and trade.ec.europa.eu/doclib/docs/2011/march/tradoc_147719.pdf. Each of these agreements includes comprehensive services and investment chapters.

88 Christian Russau, "Investment Regimes in the EU-MERCUSOR Negotiations," *Forschungs- und Dokumentationszentrum Chile-Lateinamerika*, Berlin, September 2005, www.fdcl-berlin.de/fileadmin/fdcl/Publikationen/2_InvestmentRegimes.pdf.

89 Stuart Trew, "Water and Water Services," in *Making Sense of the CETA: An Analysis of the Final Text of the Canada-European Union Comprehensive Economic and Trade Agreement*, ed. Scott Sinclair, Stuart Trew, and Hadrian Mertins-Kirkwood (Ottawa: Canadian Centre for Policy Alternatives, September 2014).

90 CETA was negotiated using a negative list approach. TiSA and TTIP negotiations involve mixed (negative and positive) approaches.

91 European Commission, "EU-Ukraine Deep and Comprehensive Free Trade Area," April 2013, trade.ec.europa.eu/doclib/docs/2013/april/tradoc_150981.pdf.

92 "ACP Private Sector Development Strategy," *BizClim*, March 2015, www.bizclim.org/en/images/structure/publication/issues_specific/BD%20BizClim%202015%20Report%20ENG_WEB.pdf.

93 The European Commission made regular donations to the facility's Multi-Donor Trust Fund II between 2004–09. Since then the Commission has made piecemeal contributions to individual projects such as a US$30 million capital funding project for Solid Waste Management in the southern West Bank. For more on the PPIAF, see www.ppiaf.org and www.ppiaf.org/page/sectors/water-and-sanitation.

94 Jaroslava Colajacomo, "The European Investment Bank in the South: In Whose Interest?," Friends of the Earth International, Campagna per la riforma della Banca Mondiale (CRBM), CEE Bankwatch and WEED e.V. (World Economy, Ecology and Development), January 2006.

95 The ECI Right2Water is one example where civil society has recently mobilized around the issue, but the focus of the initiative is on ensuring "all EU citizens enjoy the right to water and sanitation, to exclude water supply and management of water resources from internal market rules and liberalization." See www.right2water.eu.

5 Where to from here?

- **Re-politicization of trade in the EU**
- **NGOs as knowledge resisters, producers, and transformers**

For those who hope that progressive NGOs can and should bring about a more just, equitable, and inclusive world, this book told a dismal story. NGOs were unable to bring about substantive and normative policy change, despite unprecedented inclusion in the external trade policymaking process and wildly successful public campaigning. The changes that did result from NGO efforts amounted to mere "tweaking at the margins"—status quo adjustments to policy that kept legal and liberal priorities intact while failing to link the governance of trade to progressive social values, human health, or sustainable development. Cosmopolitans, in particular, will likely read this book with an equal measure of despair and derision. How can so much effort, institutional reform, and resources be expended to such limited effect?

There is a deeply entrenched cosmopolitan, democratic imperative in the EU—a commitment to providing channels for participation by non-state actors, and for enhancing public deliberation, transparency, inclusivity, and accountability of EU-level policymaking. In the area of external trade, non-state actors, especially NGOs, have experienced levels of access and participation in the policymaking process that are unmatched in other industrialized countries. Where NGOs take advantage of these opportunities, this should constitute an "easy test" for cosmopolitanism—NGOs that are embedded in the institutional fabric of the political process are most likely to bring about substantive policy change. Yet, we saw a very different pattern of empowerment unfold in the preceding cases.

NGOs improved the quality of external trade policymaking, both when they were integrated into the political process (as in the access to medicines case), and when they were mobilized and protesting on the streets and in the media (as in the water services liberalization case). This suggests that the causal link between formal political opportunities and improvements in democratic process are more tenuous than cosmopolitanism suggests. Indeed, there are clearly many roles through which NGOs can improve the input legitimacy of public policymaking beyond the state, ranging from activist to expert.

These prospects with respect to process notwithstanding, NGOs were equally unsuccessful in affecting policy change, despite their very different relationships with the formal external trade political process. NGOs were unable to convince EU policymakers to pursue policies that they believe would ensure greater access to medicines, reduce disparities in access to medicines between the global North and global South, and which would place public health concerns over intellectual property rights protection. Indeed, in the access to medicines case, the influence of NGOs over EU external trade policy actually diminished against the backdrop of burgeoning opportunities for participation in the formal political process. Similarly, EU policymakers continue to actively pursue water services liberalization in developing and least-developed countries, despite the best efforts of NGOs working on this issue.

This book has sought to show that NGO inputs are mediated by the social structure of global governance, something that is largely neglected by cosmopolitanism. Epistemes—the background knowledge, ideological and normative beliefs, and shared, intersubjective causal and evaluative assumptions about how the world works—structure patterns of empowerment in global governance. The shift from GATT to WTO cemented the legal-liberal episteme in global trade governance and thereby determined which policy options are (in)conceivable, and who has a voice and who is silenced. Epistemes endow technocrats and experts with the authority to maintain and reproduce the norms, consensual scientific knowledge, and ideological beliefs upon which they are built. They are empowered relative to other actors, including NGOs, to make authoritative interpretations of trade rules, develop standards in technical areas, and to use their specialized knowledge as the basis for the negotiation of new trade rules. The more technical or complex an issue, the more authority pools in the hands of experts and technocrats and can be insulated from public scrutiny. NGOs can influence trade policymaking and share their inputs and expertise so long as their contributions and demands fit within the parameters of the legal-liberal episteme. Policy proposals and solutions that challenge the legal-liberal episteme are incomprehensible and threatening to policymakers. Because the social identities of experts and technocrats are products of the dominant episteme, they work to legitimize and reproduce the ideas on which it is based, either by co-opting and absorbing critical voices or by marginalizing and silencing them. These are precisely the dynamics that played out in the preceding cases.

Because the EU is the best-case scenario—the political opportunities for non-state actors to participate in the trade political process are unmatched in other industrialized countries—it would be easy to conclude the book in despair over the dim prospects for NGOs to influence global trade and bring about meaningful change. However, we cannot resign ourselves to the status quo or eschew the need for deeper reform. Instead we must look for opportunities for challenging received wisdom about the prospects of trade to work for global development, deliver and safeguard public goods, and serve the needs of the world's poorest people. Indeed, NGOs working on the cases covered in this book reflect widespread concern about the failures of global trade to produce welfare gains for all.[1] Given the urgency of this situation, future research must center on three key questions. First, under what circumstances can NGOs successfully politicize and challenge the dominant epistemic foundations of global trade? Second, can NGOs act as transformative actors, become knowledge producers, and open up alternative institutional pathways, modes of thinking, and spaces for resistance in global trade governance? Third, what potential exists for the emergence of more emancipatory global trade policies from NGO advocacy? The following discussion takes stock of recent glimmers of hope.

Re-politicization of trade in the EU

The shift of attention away from the Doha Round to the negotiation of mega-regional trade agreements has re-politicized trade in unexpected ways in the EU, and to a lesser extent in the United States. NGOs, citizens, and parliamentarians, particularly at the EU and national levels, are rallying to block what they see as the most insidious elements of the proposed agreements. The inclusion of investor-to-state dispute settlement mechanisms in the Canada-EU CETA and the US-EU TTIP has sparked widespread condemnation across Europe as critics fear that corporations will hamstring governments in their attempts to regulate in the public interest. Perhaps more concerning are the provisions on horizontal regulatory convergence, which aim to achieve lowest common denominators in regulatory obligations among members of the agreement, and which threaten to place downward pressure on consumer safety, public health, and environmental standards.[2] There is also concern that the agreements will lead to significant job loss and insecurity. Moreover, critics have seized upon important work by scholars such as De Ville and Siles-Brügge who show that the potential economic benefits of agreements like the TTIP have been wildly exaggerated, particularly by the European Commission and its reliance on Computer Generated Equilibrium (CGE) models to justify the trade agreement.[3] In response, an alliance of NGOs and trade unions has launched a Stop/No TTIP campaign and is organizing citizens of the EU to take to the streets and to the media to publicize their grievances with respect to the mega-regionals.[4] They launched a European Citizens' Initiative—a right to petition the European Commission—calling for a halt to CETA and TTIP negotiations.[5] They are also aggressively lobbying members of the European Parliament in an effort to convince them to block the TTIP. These are signs that public contestation over trade policy is reaching new heights in Europe. Whether this will lead to any meaningful re-direction of the negotiations remains to be seen.

Since 2013, the Commission has held extensive public consultations on the TTIP and ISDS in response to "unprecedented public interest in the talks."[6] Aimed at dampening outrage over the secrecy of negotiations and allaying fears about the ISDS, incoming DG Trade Commissioner Cecilia Malmström launched a "transparency initiative" in November 2014 which would go beyond anything seen before in the EU. She made public the outcome of public consultations on ISDS which showed that 97 percent of respondents were opposed to its inclusion in TTIP.[7] Negotiations on ISDS were suspended while the Commission conducted the public consultation and mounted a response to public concerns. Malmström officially declassified the EU's negotiating mandate by the Council of Ministers, published several EU negotiating texts, and changed the rules of confidentiality so that all MEPs, not just the select few in INTA, could access negotiating texts. The Commission now also maintains a Twitter feed, @EU_TTIP_team, to keep the public abreast of developments in TTIP negotiations.[8]

Nevertheless, it appears as though the case of TTIP will play out much like the two cases treated in this book. DG Trade has undertaken these dramatic transparency measures in an effort to sell TTIP to critics (co-opt) and to debunk (silence) "myths" propagated by NGOs. NGOs and critical scholars claim the Commission is deflecting criticism by relying on arcane CGE modeling and "obfuscating language … that is difficult to understand for lay persons and can easily create misunderstandings."[9] Moreover, in a dramatic and controversial move, the Commission rejected the ECI in September 2014 on the basis that its demands "to repeal the negotiating mandate for the

Transatlantic Trade and Investment Partnership" and "not to conclude the Comprehensive Economic and Trade Agreement" do "not fall within the scope of the Regulation" on ECIs.[10] In response, NGOs appealed the decision in the European Court of Justice and continued with a self-organizing ECI without the permission of the European Commission, garnering more than 1.5 million signatures from a significant number of member states by June 2015, thereby exceeding the minimum level of support required to have an ECI officially approved.

Meanwhile, despite the widespread traction of the Stop/No TTIP campaign in the EU and public denouncements of the negotiations, TTIP is proceeding with only a few tweaks to the edges of the agreement—investor protection and regulatory harmonization remain at the core of the TTIP agenda. In May 2015, the Commission released a reform proposal in response to public outcry over the ISDS,[11] but it contains little of substance beyond a vague proposal to establish a permanent court.[12] No matter how loudly ISDS and deregulation are resisted, calls to gut these elements from mega-regionals or halt negotiations indefinitely are incomprehensible to DG Trade experts and technocrats. Indeed, the "deregulatory" bias is so deeply entrenched in the European Commission that former DG Trade Commissioner De Gucht referred to the agreement as "the cheapest stimulus package you can imagine,"[13] and current DG Trade Commissioner Malmström considers it a "no-brainer."[14] The TTIP is considered to be the main—possibly the only—engine for economic recovery and growth in the aftermath of the global financial crisis.

It appears as though we have yet another intractable ideological and normative standoff between NGOs and EU policymakers over external trade policy. For critics of the mega-regionals and the TTIP in particular, the only hope of substantive policy change now rests with the EP, which is currently being consulted on the negotiations and will have to assent to the trade deal once it is concluded. However, even MEPs seem poised to accept the most contested elements of TTIP. On 28 May 2015, a large majority of MEPs in the INTA—including some of the most critical Socialist MEPs—capitulated and endorsed the Commission's reform proposal as "the basis for negotiations on a new and effective system of investment protection," thereby approving, in principle, the inclusion of ISDS in the TTIP.[15] The EP was due to vote on INTA's resolution on 10 June 2015 and endorse the European Commission's TTIP negotiations. In light of a furious backlash among civil society and certain MEPs—particularly the Greens and some Socialists and Democrats—and a flood of some 200 proposed amendments by MEPs, EP President Martin Schulz pushed to postpone the vote rather than risk it being defeated. A political compromise was finally struck in the form of an ISDS amendment that appeased MEPs in the Progressive Alliance of Socialists and Democrats and the European People's Party, but which ultimately preserves the usual investor protection standards, in line with the Commission's reform proposal of May 2015.[16] On 8 July 2015, the EP passed a resolution supporting the TTIP negotiations including the ISDS, 436 to 241 with 32 abstentions, much to the dismay of critical NGOs, Green MEPs, and many others.[17] Official support from the EP was not required for the Commission to proceed with the TTIP negotiations and it is not a guarantee that it will accept the TTIP once it is concluded. However, given that the tenth round of TTIP negotiations was in full swing in Brussels at the time of writing, it seems likely that the EP will not resist the Commission's agenda, including on ISDS. What is also clear is that NGO activism has politicized and shaken up the mega-regional debate in significant ways, but they have not yet breached the ideological divide over external trade policy in the EU. In order to effect change, NGOs need to look for more radical means of challenging the dominant trade political agenda and the expert knowledge that undergirds it.

NGOs as knowledge resisters, producers, and transformers

A central contention of this book is that the epistemic foundations or "background knowledge" of global trade determines—and disciplines—who has a voice and which agendas are prioritized in trade negotiations. De-mystifying the origins, legitimacy, and structural power of expert knowledge in global trade is a first step to identifying prospects for NGOs to loosen the shackles of received wisdom.[18] The work of critical scholars such as Rorden Wilkinson, Silke Trommer, and Gabriel Siles-Brügge, in particular, illuminates how the language we use to talk about trade conveys, disciplines, and cements knowledge about trade.[19] Highly technical language, metaphors, myths, and common sense narratives all work to establish and uphold experts' monopoly over trade knowledge and empower experts to serve as gatekeepers over trade policymaking. Those who "talk the talk" are empowered, and detractors and critics are silenced. In a similar vein, Karen Tucker and Michael Strange use post-structuralist methodologies to examine how changing discursive and social contexts at the WTO reinforce patterns of inclusion and exclusion and ideas about appropriate subjects of dialogue.[20]

For these scholars, gaining and maintaining expert status requires one to assimilate and reproduce dominant forms of expert knowledge. Future research should explore the extent and circumstances under which NGOs have earned such expert status by learning and making strategic use of expert language to gain a voice in global trade. More crucially, scholars should explore whether NGOs can strategically speak expert language without reproducing the underlying perspectives and normative commitments that are inherent to it. Scholars might also look beyond the field of trade to evolving expert knowledge in other, overlapping domains such as development and environment. NGOs have played a central role in developing policy narratives around sustainable development within the UN system. Do the ideas generated in that context impact the generation and legitimation of expert knowledge in global trade governance? Do those narratives push against or potentially transform conventional wisdom about the possibilities of trade to work for global development? Another fruitful avenue for research is whether deliberations about progressive social values, human health, or sustainable development in different political arenas, which include a broader range of NGO voices, impact discourses and ideas about global trade.

Looking at the role of NGOs as knowledge producers provides insight into the potential for NGOs to challenge and reconstitute the epistemic foundations of global trade. For instance, Mathew Eagleton-Pearce traces the rise of Oxfam as a credible yet critical voice in global trade governance. By leveraging its research and expertise and by translating its alternative trade policy proposals into language that was intelligible to the global trade elite, Oxfam successfully developed a counter-narrative from within the dominant episteme.[21] Elsewhere, I have explored the emergence of a particular brand of NGO knowledge producer.[22] Responding to the failures of global trade to produce welfare gains for all, and eschewing conventional advocacy or protest strategies, embedded NGOs provide legal and technical trade-related expertise across a range of issue areas that are of primary concern to developing and least-developed countries. They engage in demand-driven advocacy to address injustices in global trade by institutionally empowering poor countries, and pushing an embedded liberalist agenda of inserting sustainable development priorities into global trade rules.

While embedded NGOs may improve the negotiating capacity of the least able in the multilateral trade system, they also tend to reinforce power asymmetries and patterns of dependence within both global trade itself and in the dominant discourses and forms of knowledge about global trade. The transformative potential of embedded NGOs is limited by their Western bias, their shoddy accountability performance, and their liberal economic bias. Similar criticisms could be leveled against Oxfam's "Make Trade Fair" campaign. Building upon these insights, scholars should further explore the conditions under which NGOs from the global North and global South can open up intellectual space for resistance and alternative policy options in global trade. Where poor countries rely on the expertise of NGOs to develop and articulate their positions in trade negotiations and disputes, scholars need to explore options for safeguarding their autonomy.

Scholars might also conduct comparative research on the transformative potential of state (IGO) and non-state (NGO) agents of global trade governance. NGOs have been somewhat influential in increasing the voice of the developing world, nullifying some of the asymmetries in political power vis-à-vis the rich world, and providing trade analysis to bolster their participation in global trade. What is less widely recognized is that IGOs, such as the South Centre and the United Nations Conference on Trade and Development (UNCTAD), actively challenge the dominant neoliberal agenda at the WTO through the provision of expert knowledge to developing and least-developed countries. Much of their work shows the potential for IGOs to help redress the inequalities in global economic governance.

In order to unpack these dynamics and elucidate more of the opportunities and constraints on NGO and IGO agency in global trade, future scholarship should compare the provision and impact of expertise: 1) by IGOs and NGOs; 2) by NGOs based in the global North and global South; 3) by universal IGOs (United Nations Development Programme, Food and Agriculture Organization, UNCTAD) and those that represent countries in the global North (OECD), the global South (South Centre, Advisory Centre on WTO Law), and a combination thereof (Commonwealth Secretariat). In addition, the growing networks between IGOs and NGOs deserve scholarly attention. Increasingly IGOs and NGOs collaborate in the provision of expert knowledge to developing and least-developed countries. Whether their combined efforts work to uphold or challenge the epistemic foundations of global trade remains unstudied. Moreover, this is an increasingly crowded field and conflicts tend to emerge when IGOs and NGOs provide competing or contradictory advice. We require better understanding of these dynamics and the various ways in which developing and least-developed countries navigate them. Also of interest is the role of emerging powers in creating and/or strengthening the provision of trade knowledge and expertise by NGOs and IGOs.

Finally, the tendency in the literature, as in this book, is to conceive of NGOs as agents of change that "act upon" the governance of global trade—from the margins, from the streets, from the bottom up—channeling the views of the "grassroots" upwards to higher-level actors as pressure groups, lobbyists for policy and normative change, and providers of analysis and expertise. The lion's share of NGO activity in global trade falls within these parameters. Yet an exclusive focus on NGOs as driving normative change from the bottom up misses important dynamics at play. NGOs are at times found to operate interdependently with the core organizations of global governance, like the WTO, such that the roles played by each are so enmeshed that they are almost analytically inseparable. Examples include the International Centre for Trade and Sustainable Development (ICTSD) and the German NGO Friedrich Ebert Stiftung (FES), both of which have developed symbiotic relationships with the WTO. In these cases, NGOs are operating as agents of governance—sometimes status quo preserving, sometimes status quo altering, but fundamental (as opposed to peripheral or secondary) to the operation of global governance.[23] In order to appreciate fully the potential for NGOs to bring about more emancipatory global trade policies, we need fuller empirical and theoretical understandings of these relationships.

Much more work remains to be done to realize the potential of NGOs to challenge and transform the epistemic foundations of global trade. We must find new and novel ways of exploring the conditions under which the dominant ideational imperative for further liberalization—one that uncritically accepts the notion that free trade is an end in itself that promotes welfare for all—can be resisted. The situation seems bleak in light of the findings in this book, but it is too important a task to be left by the wayside or in the dustbin of despair. Progressive social values, human health and welfare, and sustainable development hang in the balance. As John Maynard Keynes once said, "It is ideas, not vested interests, which are dangerous for good or evil."[24]

Notes

1 Rorden Wilkinson, *What's Wrong with the WTO and How to Fix It* (Cambridge: Polity Press, 2014).
2 Ferdi De Ville and Gabriel Siles-Brügge, *TTIP: The Truth about the Transatlantic Trade and Investment Partnership* (Bristol: Polity Press, 2015); and Gabriel Siles-Brügge and Nicolette Butler, "Regulatory Chill? Why TTIP Could Inhibit Governments from Regulating in the Public Interest," London School of Economics Policy Blog, 13 June 2015, blogs.lse.ac.uk/

usappblog/2015/06/13/regulatory-chill-why-ttip-could-inhibit-governments-f rom-regulating-in-the-public-interest/.

3 Ferdi De Ville and Gabriel Siles-Brügge, "The Transatlantic Trade and Investment Partnership and the Role of Computable General Equilibrium Modelling: An Exercise in 'Managing Fictional Expectations'," *New Political Economy* 2015, available on early view.

4 See for example, "Thousands in Germany Protest Against Europe-US Trade Deal," Reuters, 18 April 2015, www.euractiv.com/sections/trade-so ciety/thousands-across-europe-protest-against-ttip-313921.

5 "Stop-TTIP: Self-organized European Citizens' Initiative Against TTIP and CETA," *Stop-TTIP*, stop-ttip.org.

6 European Commission, "Commission to Consult European Public on Pro- visions in EU-US Trade Deal on Investment and Investor-State Dispute Settlement," Press Release, 21 January 2014, europa.eu/rapid/press-release_ IP-14-56_en.htm.

7 European Commission, "Online Public Consultation on Investment Pro- tection and Investor-to-State Dispute Settlement (ISDS) in the Transat- lantic Trade and Investment Partnership Agreement (TTIP)," *Commission Staff Working Document* SWD(2015) 3 final, trade.ec.europa.eu/doclib/ docs/2015/january/tradoc_153044.pdf.

8 "European Commission Publishes TTIP Legal Texts as Part of Transpar- ency Initiative," European Commission press release, 7 January 2015, europa.eu/rapid/press-release_IP-15-2980_en.htm.

9 The European Consumer Organization (BEUC) and Friends of the Earth (FOE), "Letter to Commissioner De Gucht: Communication of the Results of the TTIP Economic Impact Assessment," 5 May 2014, www.beuc.eu/p ublications/beuc-x-2014-036_mgo_joint_letter_to_mr_de_gucht_on_econom ic_figures-final.pdf. For additional commentary, see Ferdi De Ville and Gabriel Siles-Brügge, *TTIP: The Truth about the Transatlantic Trade and Investment Partnership* (Bristol: Polity Press, 2015).

10 European Commission, "Letter: Your Request for Registration of a Propose Citizens' Initiative Entitled 'STOP TTIP'," 10 September 2014, ec.europa. eu/citizens-initiative/public/documents/2552.

11 European Commission, "Investment in TTIP and Beyond—The Path for Reform," 5 May 2015, trade.ec.europa.eu/doclib/docs/2015/may/tradoc_ 153408.pdf.

12 For a discussion of the reform proposals, see Gabriel Siles-Brügge, Nicol- ette Butler, Emma Woodford, and Hannah McCarthy, "Transatlantic Trade and Investment Partnership: State of Play," ESRC/University of Manchester Impact Acceleration Account, Policy Briefing, 29 May 2015, www.policy. manchester.ac.uk/media/projects/policymanchester/TTIP-Policy-briefing—fi nal-version.pdf.

13 Karl De Gucht, "A European Perspective on Transatlantic Free Trade," speech delivered at the Harvard Kennedy School, 2 March 2013, europa. eu/rapid/press-release_SPEECH-13-178_en.htm.

14 Cecilia Malmström and Jonathan Hill, "Don't Believe the Anti-TTIP Hype—Increasing Trade is a No-Brainer," *The Guardian*, 16 February 2015, www.theguardian.com/commentisfree/2015/feb/16/ttip-transatlantic- trade-deal-businesses.

15 European Parliament, "Compromise Amendments on Draft Report Containing the European Parliament's Recommendations to the Commission on the Negotiations for TTIP," 28 May 2015, polcms.secure.europarl. europa.eu/cmsdata/upload/c60d0958-eed1-48af-9845-78682231492f/List%20 of%20Compromise%20Amendments.pdf.

16 Gabriel Siles-Brügge, "Q&A on TTIP," UNI Global Union, 6 July 2014, www.uniglobalunion.org/news/qa-ttip-leading-trade-expert-dr-gabriel-siles-brugge-university-manchester.

17 European Parliament, "European Parliament Resolution of 8 July 2015 Containing the European Parliament's Recommendations to the European Commission on the Negotiations for the Transatlantic Trade and Investment Partnership (TTIP) (2014/2228[INI])," P8_TA-PROV(2015)0252, 8 July 2015, www.europarl.europa.eu/sides/getDoc.do?pubRef=-//EP//NON SGML+TA+P8-TA-2015-0252+0+DOC+PDF+V0//EN.

18 Erin Hannah, James Scott, and Silke Trommer, eds, *Expert Knowledge in Global Trade* (Abingdon: Routledge, 2015).

19 Rorden Wilkinson, "Language, Power and Multilateral Trade Negotiations," *Review of International Political Economy* 16, no. 4 (2009): 597–619; Rorden Wilkinson, "Of Butcheries and Bicycles: The WTO and the 'Death' of the Doha Development Agenda," *The Political Quarterly* 83, no. 2 (2012): 395–401; Silke Trommer, "Trade Policy Communities, Expert Language and the Dehumanization of World Trade," in *Expert Knowledge in Global Trade*, ed. Erin Hannah, James Scott, and Silke Trommer (Abingdon: Routledge, 2015), 63–82; and Gabriel Siles-Brügge, "Explaining the Resilience of Free Trade: The Smoot-Hawley Myth and the Crisis," *Review of International Political Economy* 21, no. 3 (2014), 535–574.

20 Karen Tucker, "Participation and Subjectification in Global Governance: NGOs, Acceptable Subjectivities and the WTO," *Millennium: Journal of International Studies* 42, no. 2 (2014), 376–396; and Michael Strange, *Writing Global Trade Governance: Discourse and the WTO* (London: Routledge, 2013).

21 Matthew Eagleton-Pierce, "Symbolic Power and Social Critique in the Making of Oxfam's Trade Policy Research," in *Expert Knowledge in Global Trade*, ed. Erin Hannah, James Scott, and Silke Trommer (Abingdon: Routledge, 2015), 151–169.

22 Erin Hannah, "The Quest for Accountable Governance: Embedded NGOs and Demand Driven Advocacy in the International Trade Regime," *Journal of World Trade* 48, no. 2 (2014), 457–479.

23 Erin Hannah and James Scott, "Rethinking the Role of NGOs in Global Governance," paper presented at the International Studies Association Annual Convention, New Orleans, 18–21 February 2015.

24 John Maynard Keynes, *The General Theory of Employment, Interest and Money* (New York: Harcourt, 1936), 384.

Appendix

EU-level bureaucratic officials

- Thomas Morgens Christensen, Policy and Negotiations Desk Officer, DG Trade, Unit F1: Coordination of WTO, OECD, Trade-Related Assistance, GATT, and Committee 133, 21 September 2004.
- Paolo Garzotti, Acting Head of Unit, DG Trade, Directorate E—Sectoral Trade Questions and Market Access, Bilateral Trade Relations, 5 October 2004.
- Eva Kaluzynska, former Policy Desk Officer responsible for Civil Society Dialogue, DG Trade, Unit G3: Sustainable Development/ Civil Society Dialogue, 13 June 2005.
- Antti Pekka Karhunen, Project Manager responsible for EU-US relations, DG Enterprise, Unit A2: External Aspects of Enterprise Policy, 31 May 2005.
- Sabine Weyand, DG Trade, Member of Pascal Lamy's Cabinet, Responsible for Relations with European Parliament; Social Partners and NGOs; Transport; Energy; Sustainable Development; Employment and Social Affairs; Environment; European and Social Committee (ESC) until November 2004, 2 June 2005.
- Nikolaos Zaimis, Head of Unit, DG Trade, Unit F2—Dispute Settlement and Trade Barriers Regulation, 4 September 2004.

EU-level bureaucratic officials (anonymous)

- Deputy Head of Unit DG Trade, G1—Trade in Services and Investment; GATS and Investment, 8 October 2004.
- Deputy Head of Unit DG Trade, G1—Trade in Services and Investment; GATS and Investment, 14 June 2005.
- Desk Officer, DG Trade, Unit H2: New Technologies, Intellectual Property and Public Procurement, 2 February 2006.

- Desk Officer—Policy and negotiations; DG Trade, Unit F1—Coordination of WTO, OECD, Trade-Related Assistance; GATT; and 133 Committee, 12 October 2004.
- Desk Officer—Policy and negotiations; DG Trade, Unit F1—Coordination of WTO, OECD, Trade-Related Assistance; GATT; and 133 Committee, 1 June 2005.
- Desk Officer responsible for the international aspects of intellectual property, DG Trade, Unit H2: New Technologies, Intellectual Property and Public Procurement, 2 February 2006.
- Director, Secretariat-General Directorate B: Relations with Civil Society, 10 June 2005.
- Former Desk Officer responsible for international aspects of intellectual property (September 2000–June 2004); DG Trade, Unit H2: New Technologies, Intellectual Property and Public Procurement, 10 February 2006.
- Head of Unit, DG Trade Unit A2—Inter-institutional Relations and Communications Policy, 29 September 2004.
- Policy Desk Officer, DG Trade, Unit G1: Trade in Services and Investment, GATS and Investment, 8 October 2004.

EU member state representatives (anonymous)

- Permanent Member State Representative for Ireland; Member of Committee 133; Council of the European Union; Department of Enterprise, Trade and Employment Counselor, 11 October 2004.
- Permanent Member State Representative for the Netherlands, head of Economic Affairs; Chair of Committee 133 during July–December 2004 Netherlands EU Presidency, 4 October 2004.

Members of the EESC

- Jean-François Bence, Head of Division, External Relations, EESC, 23 September 2004.
- Dimitris Dimitriadis, Member of EESC, First Vice-President of the National Confederation of Hellenic Commerce, President and CEO of Business Architect consultancy firm, 11 October 2004.

Member of the EESC (anonymous)

- Member of EESC, Director of the Central Union of Agricultural Producers and Forest Owners (MTK), 29 September 2004.

EU industry representatives

- Pascal Kerneis, Director of the European Services Forum, 24 September 2004.
- Pascal Kerneis, Managing Director of the European Services Forum, 15 June 2005.
- Shelby Matthews, Director International Affairs, Agri Producers— Comité des Organisations Professionnelles Agricoles de l'Union Européenne & Comité Général de la Coopération Agricole de l'Union Européenne (COPA-COGECA), 11 October 2004.
- Peter McNamee, Legal Advisor, Council of Bars and Law Societies of Europe (CCBE), 10 June 2005.
- Marc Pouw, Secretary-General, Association of European Public Postal Operators (PostEurop), phone interview by author, 1 July 2005.
- Mark van der Horst, Chairman, Competition and Market Reform Committee, European Express Association (EEA), 7 June 2005.

EU industry representatives (anonymous)

- Advisor/Advocacy Officer/lawyer, European Foreign Trade Association (EFTA), phone interview by author, 27 September 2004.
- Director of the International Relations Department, WTO Advisor, Union of Industrial and Employers' Confederations of Europe (UNICE), 24 September 2004.
- Strategy Analyst, ERT, 7 October 2004.
- Trade policy advisor, Union of Electricity Industry—Eurelectric, 3 June 2005.

Trade union representatives

- Peter Coldrick, former Confederal Secretary of the European Trade Union Confederation, 18 May 2005.
- James Howard, Director for Employment and Special Labour Standards, International Confederation of Free Trade Unions, 9 June 2005.

NGO representatives

- Louis Belanger, OXFAM International: EU Advocacy and Media Officer, 8 February 2006.

- Jennifer Brant, International Trade Analyst, Sidley Austin LLP, formerly a Trade Policy Advisor with Oxfam America, interview by author in Geneva, Switzerland, 24 February 2006.
- Seco Gerard, Access Campaign EU Liaison Officer, Médecins Sans Frontières (MSF), 9 February 2006.
- Guillame Legaut, Trade and Food Security Advocacy Officer, Development, Coopération Internationale pour le Développement et la Solidarité (CIDSE), 2 June 2005.
- Marc Maes, European Policy Officer, Coalition of the Flemish North South Movement 11.11.11, 6 June 2005.
- Stijn Oosterlynck, Advocacy Officer, Attac-Flanders, 18 May 2005.
- Erik Wesselieus, Campaigner and Researcher at Corporate European Observatory and GATSwatch, 23 May 2004.

NGO representatives (anonymous)

- Deputy General Secretary, European Federation of Public Service Unions (EPSU), phone interview by author, 10 May 2005.
- European Trade Policy Officer, WWF, 4 October 2004.

Index

Routledge Global Institutions Series

Books currently under contract include:

The Regional Development Banks
Lending with a regional flavor
by Jonathan R. Strand (University of Nevada)

Millennium Development Goals (MDGs)
For a people-centered development agenda?
by Sakiko Fukada-Parr (The New School)

The Bank for International Settlements
The politics of global financial supervision in the age of high finance
by Kevin Ozgercin (SUNY College at Old Westbury)

International Migration
by Khalid Koser (Geneva Centre for Security Policy)

The International Monetary Fund (2nd edition)
Politics of conditional lending
by James Raymond Vreeland (Georgetown University)

The UN Global Compact
by Catia Gregoratti (Lund University)

Institutions for Women's Rights
*by Charlotte Patton (York College, CUNY) and
Carolyn Stephenson (University of Hawaii)*

International Aid
by Paul Mosley (University of Sheffield)

Coping with Nuclear Weapons
by W. Pal Sidhu

Global Governance and China
The dragon's learning curve
edited by Scott Kennedy (Indiana University)

The Politics of Global Economic Surveillance
by Martin S. Edwards (Seton Hall University)

Mercy and Mercenaries
Humanitarian agencies and private security companies
by Peter Hoffman

Regional Organizations in the Middle East
by James Worrall (University of Leeds)

Reforming the UN Development System
The Politics of Incrementalism
by Silke Weinlich (Duisburg-Essen University)

The International Criminal Court
The Politics and practice of prosecuting atrocity crimes
by Martin Mennecke (University of Copenhagen)

BRICS
*by João Pontes Nogueira (Catholic University, Rio de Janeiro) and
Monica Herz (Catholic University, Rio de Janeiro)*

The European Union (2nd edition)
Clive Archer (Manchester Metropolitan University)

Protecting the Internally Displaced
Rhetoric and reality
Phil Orchard (University of Queensland)

For further information regarding the series, please contact:

Nicola Parkin, Editor, Politics & International Studies
Taylor & Francis
2 Park Square, Milton Park, Abingdon
Oxford OX14 4RN, UK
Nicola.parkin@tandf.co.uk
www.routledge.com

For Product Safety Concerns and Information please contact our EU
representative GPSR@taylorandfrancis.com Taylor & Francis Verlag GmbH,
Kaufingerstraße 24, 80331 München, Germany

Printed and bound by CPI Group (UK) Ltd, Croydon, CR0 4YY
08/05/2025
01864358-0004